BULLY OFF

Recognising and tackling workplace bullying

Jo Clifton and Heather Serdar

Russell House Publishing

Bully Off: Recognising and tackling workplace bullying

First published in 2000 by:
Russell House Publishing Ltd
4 St. George's House
Uplyme Road
Lyme Regis
Dorset DT7 3LS
Tel: 01297 443948
Fax: 01297 442722
e-mail: help@russellhouse.co.uk

© Jo Clifton and Heather Serdar

The right of Jo Clifton and Heather Serdar to be identified as authors of this work has been asserted by them in accordance with the Copyright, Designs and Patent Act 1988.

All rights reserved. No part of this publication may be reproduced, stored in a retrieval system or transmitted in any form, or by any means, electronic, mechanical, photocopying, recording or otherwise, without the prior permission of the copyright holder and the publisher.

British Library Cataloguing-in-Publication Data:
A catalogue record for this book is available from the British Library.

ISBN: 1-898924-66-X

Design and layout by: Jeremy Spencer, London

Printed by Redwood Books, Trowbridge

Russell House Publishing

is a group of social work, probation, education and youth and community work practitioners and academics working in collaboration with a professional publishing team. Our aim is to work closely with the field to produce innovative and valuable materials to help managers, trainers, practitioners and students. We are keen to receive feedback on publications and new ideas for future projects.

Contents

Thanks

The experiences related in this book are still having enormous effects on the targets. For some, the misery is continuing and so our thanks are recorded here for their courage in sharing their experiences for the benefit of others.

For examples of Good Practice and permission to give details of their training and practice to promote a Positive Culture within the workplace, we would also like to thank:

Fife Council
City of Hull Council
Cambridge Housing Association

Thanks also to Susi Petherick, who was to have been one of the authors, but in the middle of the research, got whisked away to Perth in Australia!

Jo Clifton
Heather Serdar

About the authors

Jo Clifton is an independent trainer and consultant who runs workshops on workplace bullying, personal development, assertiveness, positive thinking and other issues.

Heather Serdar writes in the introduction … 'My involvement in the book was due to the fact that I had been been bullied while working in a previous job. I have moved on, both professionally and personally; I hope my colleague has too.'

For those of you with access to the internet, you may be interested in the site we are currently setting up to promote interest in addressing this issue. You will find us at Bullyoff.com

Introduction

Why have we written this book?

This book came to be written as a result of the separate experiences of each of the authors. One impetus came from the assertiveness and positive thinking workshops Jo Clifton was running around the UK. She realised that an alarming number of people were attending the workshops with horrific stories of the behaviour of colleagues, or more usually, of their managers.

These examples went far beyond the usual types of unconscious unassertive or even aggressive behaviour, which is present in many workplaces. The disconcerting feature of these examples was the feeling by the participant that it was somehow their fault and if only they were more assertive, they would be able to deal with it.

Although working on confidence building and personal development issues is a significant support in helping to deal with the bullying, the majority of those participants were too damaged to benefit from the group-based approach. Fellow trainers, especially those delivering stress management workshops, had also contributed similar examples of damage to individuals.

In order to gauge the interest in running a workshop specifically for people experiencing bullying, we negotiated with Dundee University to run a pilot session as part of their Lifelong Learning Programme.

Although the maximum numbers had been set at 12, the rate of applications persuaded the university to raise the numbers and it was finally closed at 18 participants working with two facilitators. The workshop is now a permanent fixture in the university calendar, but is now separated into *Identifying and Tackling Workplace Bullying*, for employers, managers etc., and *Dealing with Workplace Bullying*, for those with personal experience of being bullied.

At the pilot workshop it was decided that whilst bully was an suitable term, *victim* was deemed inappropriate, as this suggested an incidental happening. The decision was taken to use the term *target* as this more prominently highlighted the negative intent and focus of the bully's behaviour. This term has been used throughout this publication except where it is used in quotes and examples contributed by third persons.

Heather Serdar writes:

> *My original reason for co-writing this book with Jo Clifton was not out of professional interest but personal experience. My involvement in the book was due to the fact that I had been bullied while working overseas.*

At the time, I had not read anything on bullying in the workplace and simply did not know that such a thing existed. I put what happened to me as the target of a serially bullying colleague, down to bad management and cultural differences. My response was the all-too-common one that it must be me and, therefore, it was up to me to make the situation better? Of course, despite my best efforts, the situation did not change.

Writing this book has been a sort of catharsis for me. As far as I know, the bully still works for the same company in the same position. I, however, have moved on both professionally and emotionally.

I would like to say to anyone who has been, or is currently, the target of a bully, you are not a victim. You are not alone. Have courage, there are remedies and steps you can take to change the situation.

Who did we write it for?

The book is designed:

- To help individuals who are concerned that they may be the target of a bully to:
  - recognise that it is happening to them
  - find support and advice to de-escalate tensions
  - equip themselves to continue positively at work
  - safeguard themselves from the effects of bullying
- To help employers and managers to develop a healthy workplace by:
  - recognising bullying at work
  - differentiating between bullying and management
  - responding effectively when it happens
  - setting up effective systems to prevent future occurrences

Use of case studies

Individuals and organisations taking part in a small survey undertaken during 1999 have provided examples of specific instances of bullying and their own methods of tackling the problem. The names and circumstances of the individuals who have had personal experience of bullying have been altered, in order to respect confidentiality.

Background

What is bullying?

Bullying can be defined as:

Persistent, offensive, abusive, intimidating, malicious or insulting behaviour, abuse of power or unfair penal sanctions, which make the recipient feel upset, threatened, humiliated or vulnerable, which undermines their self-confidence and which may cause them to suffer stress.

(MSFU, 1994)

The continual and relentless attack on other people's self-confidence and self esteem in an intentional, regular and repeated manner.

(Unknown)

...the aggressive behaviour arising from the deliberate attempt to cause physical or psychological distress to others.

(Peter Randall, 1996)

Raising the issue

Although it is not a new phenomenon, the issue of workplace bullying was first brought to prominence in 1992 by Andrea Adams through two BBC Radio 4 documentaries: *An Abuse of Power* and *Whose Fault is it Anyway?*

These programmes received an amazing response from people all over the country, whose lives had been made intolerable by being bullied at work. To further highlight the issue, Adams produced a book, *Bullying at Work*, in conjunction with Neil Crawford, which sparked off research and a series of conferences and seminars, often instigated by trades unions. The outcome of these investigations showed the issue to be far more widespread than previously thought.

Raising the profile

In May 1994, The Manufacturing, Science and Finance Union held a conference entitled *Bullying at Work*, to raise awareness of the problem. Their use of the word 'bullying' gave a new insight into what was happening to many of their members throughout the UK.

In 1996, The Institute of Personnel and Development, surveying a thousand people, found that one person in eight had been bullied in the past five years, extrapolating to two million people in Britain as a whole. Furthermore, they found that over half of those who have experienced bullying say it is commonplace in their organisation and a quarter believed it had got worse in the last year.

Additionally, a similar piece of research from Staffordshire University Business School indicated that 53 per cent, around 14 million, of UK employees have been bullied at work during their working life.

In December 1997, the Trades Union Congress, (TUC), operated a *Bad Bosses Hotline*, offering employees the opportunity to express concerns about the conditions in their workplace. The hotline logged an overwhelming five thousand calls in five days, with a significant number of callers being of middle management level.

Well ahead of low pay, contracts, long hours, unfair dismissal, health and safety, etc., the largest number of calls, 38 per cent, concerned bullying.

In 1996, Tim Field, author of *Bully in Sight*, started the UK National Workplace Bullying Advice Line and has logged over three thousand cases of bullying to date. During this time, he has been instrumental in keeping the issue to the fore, devoting most of his time to raising awareness of the damaging effects of bullying in the workplace. Of the calls he has received, surprisingly, the largest number are from employees in the 'caring sector', with 20 per cent from Education, 12 per cent from the NHS and 10 per cent from Social Work.

During 1998, furthermore, the largest growing employment category of callers was from the voluntary and non-profit sector. Some of the worst cases involved charities that care for emotionally, sexually and physically abused children, together with social housing, especially involving elderly people.

Research

Findings from studies and research have also suggested that certain environmental conditions and organisational structures can actually encourage bullying behaviour and a bullying culture. These include:

- Lack of job security.
- Increased pressure on managers to reach targets, often with a reduced work force.
- No policy or structure for resolving interpersonal issues and conflict.
- Lack of training in management, supervisory or interpersonal skills.

Bullying, harassment and discrimination

Bullying differs from harassment and discrimination in that the focus in bullying is rarely based on gender, race, or disability. Indeed, the focus is often on competence or popularity, which the bully will then attempt to undermine by negative behaviour.

There is also an absence of the physical element that is such a feature of harassment and this often prevents the target from being initially aware of the bullying. It is more often a build-up of small and seemingly trivial incidents and behaviours that characterises the bullying. As it is less easily recognised, the target can be subject to the negative behaviour for as much as several years without realising the cause of their resulting loss of confidence. This can also impact on the competence and performance of the target, who is aware of the result, but very seldom aware of the cause.

Whilst bullying may be seen as the common denominator of all harassment, discrimination, abuse, conflict and violence, bullying by itself varies from harassment and discrimination in many ways, such as the frequency and duration of the actions. Because of this, initiatives to address these issues of harassment and discrimination, will need to have a separate section solely devoted to bullying. The causes, the perpetrator's motives, and the tactics are different and there are also many different types of bullying, which will need to be identified in order for an appropriate solution to be decided.

Bullying or not?

How are we then to determine whether certain behaviour constitutes bullying? Can someone bully without intending to? Who decides that it is bullying and not just inappropriate management styles?

The target

For the target of bullying, it may be necessary to analyse and reflect on the situation at work, by asking such questions as:

- Does my workload seem excessive in comparison to others in my organisation or team?
- Do I feel that I have less support than my colleagues have in similar circumstances, or even that I receive no support at all?
- Am I given less time to complete my tasks than comparable ones given to colleagues?
- Am I asked to be more accountable than others in the workplace?
- Are there continual changes to my targets or workloads with little or no notice?

There is no really foolproof way of recognition beyond doubt that bullying is the cause. However, one way may be to consider the feelings experienced by the target, and the effect it has on them, with some effects being visible and capable of measurement, whilst others are more difficult to define.

Does the target *feel* bullied? Or if they have not identified the behaviour with that particular label, do they have feelings of being constantly humiliated, systematically devalued or treated in such a way that they experience real fear either in the workplace or in the thought of being there?

The organisation

Is the management system in operation one that supports its staff or is it one that could create a climate where some people feel free to humiliate, frighten and degrade other individuals? It is accepted that workplaces need to involve systems and procedures where standards and targets are set, monitored and maintained.

Failure to achieve these targets is a legitimate cause for concern by management and colleagues alike and these will obviously require highlighting and remedial action taken. In addition, responsible managers will be alive to the various abilities and talents of their workers and will encourage high standards, but, with pressure on themselves to perform and fulfil organisational goals, they may exhibit isolated incidents of negative behaviour.

Therefore, it is important that distinctions are made between structured management, when the regime is quite strict, and a systematic and persistent catalogue of abuse of power. Isolated incidents and 'legitimate' criticism would not normally be viewed as bullying, while persistent undermining and abusive behaviour could be. For example, one manager received 42 memos in one day containing trivial criticisms from his chief executive as part of a campaign of bullying.

Tactics of bullying may also include undermining the authority of the target, constantly changing priorities, for instance, without informing them, leaving them confused and de-motivated – effectively isolating them and making it easier for the bully to continue their regime of terror.

Giving it a name

Initially the target may be unaware that there is a deliberate negative intent behind the instructions or criticisms. They progressively try harder to please the bully, but with no success, since the bully is not looking for legitimate improvement or the attainment of corporate goals. By manipulating the situation, they are also manipulating the target. That's not management; that's control!

In all cases it is vital to identify this behaviour as bullying and not, as journalist Polly Toynbee wrote in 1999, in the *Radio Times*, 'a functional part of the workplace'. Toynbee claimed that people were bullied because they were under-performing and unpopular with colleagues. She felt it was kinder for them to be bullied out of work than go through the humiliation of being sacked.

Research shows that the majority of targets, far from under-performing, often have a high degree of skills, an excellent work record, pleasant personalities and are popular with others, until the bully targets them for attention.

At present, there is not a single law that can seek to prevent bullying in the workplace, although campaigns are being waged by trades unions, professional bodies and concerned individuals. With their combined strength and determination of purpose, we may yet provide a workplace where people feel valued and secure rather than oppressed and fearful.

The Dignity at Work Bill, (1997), formulated by MSF Union, was presented to the House of Lords. It moved successfully through that House, but then fell because it did not receive sufficient parliamentary time under the previous administration.

Section 1

The Individual Perspective

Chapter 1

The Target

Identifying the issues

As defined earlier, and in this context, the 'target' is 'the deliberate object of a bully's negative attentions'.

How to recognise bullying behaviour: the outward and initial signs

Because there is now a greater emphasis on reaching set performance criteria and achieving corporate and individual goals, there is increased pressure in the workplace on managers and supervisors to reach targets. This pressure may also affect the way that people behave towards each other and how individuals respond to the situation. However, there will also be, within any workplace, the potential for intentional negative behaviour. In a culture where a 'fault and blame' situation exists, or where people are untrained or inexperienced, the bully can instigate a reign of terror and hide behind excuses of 'just getting the job done'.

Do you feel that you may be experiencing bullying behaviour? Can you recognise any or all or the elements within this chapter? The important thing is, do you feel bullied, even if you've never actually given it that particular name? The following signs, symptoms and indications will be a pretty good measure of judging whether you are, in fact, the target of a bully, and, having acknowledged this, you can start to tackle the problem.

Are you experiencing excessive pressure from your manager or supervisor, or possibly your colleagues, by any of these methods?

- **Continual fault-finding and criticism of a trivial nature:** It is the triviality, regularity and frequency that identifies this behaviour as bullying. Added to that is the absence of any opportunity to discuss and resolve these criticisms. The bully may even choose some triviality, which could be seen as having some validity and, if your confidence levels are very low, this could actually fool you into believing the whole criticism, which will reduce your will to refute it.

- **Contributions and achievements are constantly refused recognition:** No matter what standard of work you produce, it is never good enough. An insidious variation of this, is that after refusing recognition to you, the bully will plagiarise or even steal your ideas and claim them as their own.

- **Continually undermining you and your position:** The bully countermands instructions, openly criticising you to colleagues and subordinates.

- **Being singled out and treated differently:** Being the only one asked to complete detailed time-logs, or selected when inappropriate tasks are being handed out, such as cleaning the toilet.

- **Being subjected to disciplinary procedures:** With verbal or written warnings imposed for trivial or fabricated reasons and without proper investigation.
- **Being isolated and separated from colleagues:** Possibly physically, such as being made to move your desk or office from the centre of the operation.
- **Being denied essential information:** Such as information that everyone at a similar grade or position is being given.
- **Being humiliated:** The bully shouts and threatens you, often in front of others, or they may make patronising and belittling comments.
- **Having your workload changed:** Work and authority being removed, being overloaded with work or responsibility with little or no extra support or authority to carry it out, or being given only menial tasks such as filing, photocopying etc., that are inappropriate to your work grade.
- **Being set unrealistic goals which change as you approach them:** The same often happens with deadlines, which are changed at short notice, or no notice, and without you being informed about it until it's too late.

Is this bullying?

Any of these aspects, in isolation, may indicate that you are the target of ineffective or unsupportive management and the resolution of the problems lie in other areas.

However, if this 'mis-management' was of a long duration or all of the aspects were present concurrently, it would certainly be characteristic of bullying behaviour. And if, added to this, you were given no opportunity to discuss the difficulties or were actively discouraged from having them resolved, it could be presented as a case of bullying. These aspects would also point to organisational deficiencies as well as individual bad practice.

> *Paula was a junior member of staff of a voluntary organisation, working in the head office as an administrative assistant. She knew herself to stand out a little with her brightly coloured hair and nose rings. However, she seemed to be integrated into the staff group who smiled at her appearance, but otherwise had no problems with it. She was totally unprepared for the reaction of the new senior manager who intimated that her appearance meant she wasn't to be trusted and that she would 'have to be watched'. This 'watching' took the form of a demand that Paula filled in a 10 minute time log each and every day. 'I thought, at first, that everyone was doing it, but then I realised it was just me. No one gave me any reason for it. I don't think anyone even looked at it, it was just to prove to me that they had power over me.'*

As well as an excess of control over work practices such as in Paula's case, some targets find that the bully likes to 'keep them in their place' or make them unsure of themselves by making strange and often wild accusations about them.

> *Jenny's manager, after repeated attempts to undermine her confidence by making unsubstantiated criticisms on her performance, called her in to the office to complain that she 'walked inappropriately'. And on another occasion, that she 'burst into song' when walking along the corridor. Jenny was finding it hard to deal with the situation as it*

became almost surreal. Each criticism seemed trivial on its own and would, she felt, be laughed at had she complained to someone higher in authority. She began to be increasingly conscious about what she did and how she performed even the simplest of tasks or activities. Things that she had previously done with no thought or effort, now took an immense effort.

It became very significant at one point, when she returned from a day off, to be told that she had to sit an exam in ten minutes, the results of which would ' have a bearing on her continued employment.' When she looked over the exam papers, she noticed that they had been sent over a week previously and so it would have been reasonable to have been given notice of having to complete it.

The impact of bullying: general symptoms

Loss of confidence

Although we are all individuals who have different perceptions and different thresholds of tolerance and awareness, there are certain symptoms that seem to be common to all targets of bullies. The most immediate effect seems to be loss of confidence and this can manifest itself in many ways.

Anna found that it was becoming increasingly difficult to make a decision, especially one that would ultimately bring her to the attention of her boss. Whenever she was faced with making a choice or giving an opinion, she would find her mind becoming quite blank and a situation akin to panic would wash over her. She would start to shake and lose control of her breathing.

She began to doubt her own ability to do the job, feeling that, because she had returned to her present job after a long break to bring up her children, she was probably 'past it'.

Increase in stress levels

The bullying can cause a fight or flight reaction in you, which means you will tense up and start to breathe from your chest rather than from your diaphragm. This chest breathing is useful during vigorous exercise, but when performed at rest, can cause feelings of anxiety and tension.

Because you are reacting, rather than responding, you may become so over stressed, a condition known as hypervigilance, that judgement becomes seriously impaired.

The intensity of the stress generated by the bullying behaviour will significantly affect how well or badly you perform. It is a vicious circle, where the bullying reduces your will or your ability to effectively handle or resolve the situation. (See Figure 1 on the next page).

People who have been bullied often speak of feeling that they are losing their mind, where they forget things, or freeze at the sound or sight of the bully.

'I just couldn't understand what was going on', said one target, 'I used to be so confident and outgoing. Now I was feeling sick at the thought of work. My boss only had to look at me and I started to shake. It was just like being a small child caught out in some misdemeanour'.

Figure 1: The stress curve

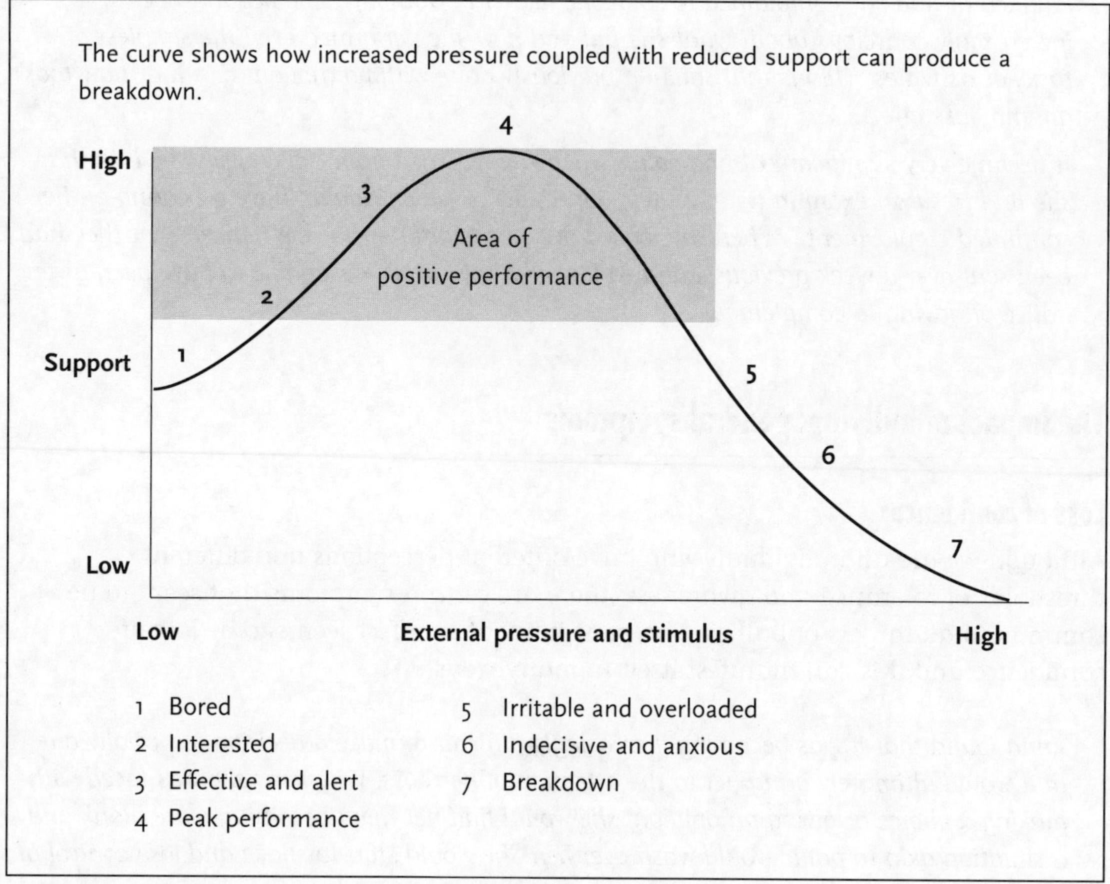

Reduction in performance

One noticeable aspect may be a tendency to under-perform in tasks and activities where previously you were able to handle and possibly excel at them. Tasks that you are now finding beyond you. Or perhaps you still feel that you are maintaining the standard but you are being 'marked down' by your manager or supervisor at appraisals or supervision sessions.

Inability to make decisions

Because of their experiences with the bully, the target's ability to think clearly and rationally is often affected. They feel that they will be blamed for whatever decision they make, and so try to delay making the decision and, therefore, the consequences of the decision.

If decision making is an integral part of a work plan, this can have a 'knock-on' effect on the performance and achievements of both the target and their colleagues. Their indecision will, therefore, impact on the work of the team, aggravating any potential conflict and resulting in further isolation of the target.

Obsession with the bully

The target becomes obsessed with the bully and the bullying, including the natural desire to resolve the conflict, and can think or talk of nothing else. This can have the effect of creating an inability to focus on the work in hand, thereby causing a drop in performance and results.

It may also alienate friends and colleagues who cannot understand this obsession since, even at this stage, the target may not have confided their problem to others.

Out of character behaviour

The target can be so much on edge that they behave quite differently from usual. Quiet and passive characters may suddenly have outbursts of anger at inappropriate times, or, from being outgoing and gregarious, they may become secretive, and withdraw from the usual group activities. This can be the start of the isolation of the target from their usual colleagues, with a resulting reduction in accessibility to support systems.

Constant approval seeking

Being so nervous of the reaction that their work will invoke in the bully, a target may constantly seek reassurance from colleagues or even the bully themselves that 'everything is OK'. They will often need to have each piece of work approved before they can move on to the next stage. There will be little initiative or creativity shown, sticking with the safe, if uninspiring, standards. This can then confirm the bully's statements about the poor performance of the target.

This behaviour may also include offering to take on more work than others or to stay later to finish pieces of work.

Poor time-keeping

Because the target may dread going to the workplace, they find little motivation to get to work on time. The lateness may also be because the physical symptoms, such as sleeplessness and the resulting fatigue, may make it impossible to drag themselves from bed or prepare themselves for work. This is another of the 'self-fulfilling prophesies', where the bully's accusations of unreliability (like poor time-keeping) is shown to be correct.

The impact of bullying: physical symptoms

Because bullying can be subtle, you may be unaware that the symptoms you are experiencing are as a direct result of the bullying behaviour. However, you will be aware that certain symptoms are manifesting themselves. The following are a selection of the most common, and immediate, symptoms to appear:

- sleeplessness, resulting in fatigue
- tearfulness
- irritability
- headaches
- high blood pressure
- palpitations
- stomach/bowel problems
- minor aches and pains
- sweating

Any one of these symptoms or a combination of them, may result in small illnesses or a general feeling of being unwell. These small illnesses, in their turn, will affect your strength to tackle the situation.

You may find that some of the symptoms manifest themselves at home and may, therefore, be less easy to connect with what is happening at work.

> *Andrew found himself feeling increasingly tired, although he seemed to be going to bed earlier than usual and sleeping later. He cut down dramatically on his social life, giving up the photography night classes that he had been so enthusiastic about previously. He recognised later that his motivation to further his interests had almost disappeared. 'Looking back, I realised that it was part of the campaign of making me feel stupid. She, the bully, had made many disparaging remarks about the evening class. At my annual appraisal, when I mentioned that I would like to advance my interest in photography professionally, she had said, 'Not really a job for a man is it?'. After that, she lost no opportunity to belittle both the classes and my ability to do anything worthwhile.*

The impact of bullying: emotional symptoms

The sense of 'why me?'

When the target becomes aware of the effects, and possibly starts to recognise the causes, other symptoms begin to appear and to affect them emotionally. They ask themselves, 'Why is this happening to me?' or 'What have I done for the bully to pick on me?'

Questions such as these, of course, seldom have any rational answer and the target may then move on to the next stage of blaming themselves. They cannot understand why they are not strong enough to deal with the situation. The confidence that has slowly been ebbing away, now retreats into a significant feeling of low self-worth and perhaps a confirmation that the bully is right to behave in that way.

The sense of vulnerability

Once the target has recognised or acknowledged the fact that they are being bullied, feelings of insecurity may arise about possible job loss. If the target is the major, or sole, wage earner in the family, fears of being unable to pay the mortgage or any bills add to the target's fragile emotional state and compound the feeling of low self-esteem.

The sense of isolation

One of the tactics employed by a bully is to manipulate the situation to where the target is isolated from the support, resources and information that are available to their colleagues. Because of the trauma that the target is experiencing, they may behave in a way that also alienates them from their colleagues. This sense of isolation is compounded by the feelings of low self-worth and the thought that no one cares enough to intervene. The target may then *choose* to keep away from their colleagues, and the isolation becomes complete.

The sense of injustice

Because of the isolation of the target, a heightened sense of injustice may now become paramount. At times of stress, we can find ourselves falling into a 'child-like' state where we want someone, the adult, to deal with the situation, and questions like 'Why doesn't anyone do anything?', 'Why doesn't anyone stand up and help me?', 'Don't they see what is happening?' and 'Don't they care what happens to me?' present themselves.

If the target feels they are being marginalised, they may then become resentful of their colleagues, their manager, in fact everyone who seems to be totally ignoring the situation.

The sense of powerlessness

With confidence being eroded and continual humiliation as a significant part of the working day, the target can start to adopt a victim mentality. In the target's perception, the responsibility for the bullying shifts from the bully to themselves, and thoughts like, 'Because I am worthless, I brought this on myself, I deserve this, I am a failure, I can't do anything right' and 'No one is able to help me and I have no power to help myself' can occur.

Whilst these thoughts are overwhelming, the target can see no way of resolving the situation, but may instead be working out ways of removing themselves, by resignation, in the best scenario, or by suicide, in the worst.

This is obviously a very significant stage and one where the most damage is visible. It is also the stage that will take the greatest time to recover from.

The impact of bullying: other symptoms

As the target continues to experience extreme stress, it may also manifest itself in other symptoms such as:

- apathy
- anxiety
- poor concentration and memory
- panic attacks
- suicidal thoughts
- chest pains
- post-traumatic stress disorder
- negativism
- increased susceptibility to illness
- mood swings

Which may lead on to:

- increased consumption of alcohol
- drug dependency
- eating disorders

- withdrawal
- loss of libido
- suicide

Once the psychological or psychiatric trauma has been sustained, then without intervention and support, the target's emotional state goes down in a spiral. The target may become increasingly withdrawn and isolated.

They become afraid that expressing what has happened to them will bring further criticism, ridicule or even retribution from the bully, thus increasing their inability to operate.

The target may then become dependent on alcohol or anti-depressants to dull these feelings, making it even more difficult for them to communicate their concerns and thus isolating them even further.

Tackling the bullying

Bullying is a conscious act, which affects everyone around it. But, because it often happens through small and almost unrelated incidents, you may not connect what is happening with the effect that it is having.

Initially, you may be unaware that there is a deliberately negative intent behind the bully's behaviour. It may seem as though they just have very high standards and somehow you are not reaching them, or that perhaps you are upsetting them in some way. You try progressively harder to please the bully, but with no success. You may also feel that you are the only person experiencing this, and perhaps it is the over-used 'personality clash'.

Once you have identified that what is happening is inappropriate behaviour, the first step should always be to identify and report the situation. However, as it is often difficult to recognise the experience as bullying until well into the situation, you may have lost all confidence in yourself and feel extremely vulnerable. You may feel that your only options are either to go on sick leave or resign from the organisation. Some people may feel strong enough to address the problem themselves, but it is vital that it is not tackled alone.

Addressing the problem

Keep a record

As soon as you are aware of what is happening, begin to record all instances of the bullying behaviour, but *remember to keep these safe, preferably not in the workplace*. Note the actual incident including:

- The date, time and location.
- Exactly what was said or done.
- All relevant background information. For instance, was it a busy time, was there an emergency, was it a quiet period, had you or the bully just come back from holiday or just about to go off on one.
- Record how you felt, before, during and after the incident.

- Identify who was involved and what part they played in the incident, even if they were just around and had witnessed it. You may wish to speak to them subsequently to see if their recollection matches yours.
- You may also wish to ask for an agreement that they would support you if you wish to take this further. However, remember that they may be reluctant to do this if they feel it would jeopardise their own position.
- Obtain a copy of your job description and see if it accurately matches the job you do.
- Retain all copies of memos, e-mails and so on that support evidence of the bullying behaviour.
- Record, or keep, all instances and evidence of positive feedback from other managers and supervisors etc. Ask for evidence of their experience of your work and performance.

Analyse the record

- Does it happen on a certain time of day, week, month etc.?
- Are the same people involved?
- Does it follow a particular event?
- Is there a pattern?

Tell someone in your family

If you are experiencing stress from a work-based problem, which is going to affect your health and behaviour at home, these effects are going to be noticed by your family. Keeping the problems to yourself and not explaining the cause may start to produce difficulties in home relationships. This could result in you experiencing stress in both places, and, without a strong support base at home, you will find it extremely difficult to deal with the problem at work.

It is vital that you are able to talk about the effects of the bullying behaviour with someone you trust. This will give you an opportunity to be as open as possible and to be able to identify that what is happening is not your fault.

Tell someone at work

Management support

The logical person is your line manager, so tell them about the behaviour and how it makes you feel. Resist the urge to use emotive language, like 'She's just a rotten bitch', but be sure to use the word bullying. If your manager is the person doing the bullying, can you by-pass them? Is there a procedure that provides a route to someone above them? Is there provision in your conditions of service to go over the boss's head to their boss?

You will need to decide what you are going to say to your manager. Are you making a formal complaint, or just bringing it to their attention. Remember that there are certain things that your manager cannot fail to pass on to a higher authority, so be clear about what you want the manager to know and to do.

Organisational support

Contact your human resources department: Can you speak to someone in that department about the problem? Are there are anti-harassment and bullying policies or procedures in force? Are there trained and experienced 'support staff that you can contact?

Investigate other policies and procedures: Are there support policies such as a grievance policy, which could help you take this forward?

Check your contract or terms and conditions: Is there any indication in them about what constitutes inappropriate behaviour and what you should do in the event of this behaviour being evident? Remember, there is an implied term within your contract, which gives you certain rights not to be discriminated against, and bullying is a form of discrimination! Your employer also has a 'duty of care' towards you as an employee.

Contact occupational health: Bullying causes prolonged negative stress and psychiatric injury. You are unlikely to be the only person to contact your OH department – and you may not be the first to name the bully.

Contact your welfare and counselling officer: Remember, a traumatic experience such as being bullied may cause past traumas to surface and become part of the ongoing situation.

Union support

Do you know where your union stands on bullying and harassment? Ask if there is a written policy on these issues. If you are a member of a union, you are entitled to help and support regarding your working conditions. Is there a shop steward or union representative you can contact for advice? They should also be able to offer support when you meet with other parties to raise or try to resolve the situation.

Even if you aren't in the union, they may still be able to give you advice although they may not be able to represent you. Remember that the bully may be in a union. Can you contact them to complain about the behaviour of one of their members?

Peer support

Tell someone you trust. They may have spotted the bullying and be willing to support you if you need to make an official complaint. Even if they have not noticed the bullying, they may have noticed the changes that have happened to you. If your behaviour has been unusual or erratic, it may have prevented your colleagues offering the support that you needed. By confiding in them, you give them a chance to help.

If you are being bullied, there may be others experiencing it as well. If you have the opportunity, observe how other people are behaving. Do you recognise your own symptoms in others' behaviour? Are other people looking tense and frightened? You may be able to confide in them and share your experiences so that there is a stronger case to take to complaint, and which helps to overcome the accusation of a 'personality clash'.

Investigate sources of external help

Visit your doctor

Tell your doctor why you are feeling as you are. If you continue with your case and take it to tribunal, you will need evidence that the situation was bad enough to seek medical help. If you think it will help, ask the doctor for a note spelling out the reason for your visit and include that with your 'sick note' to your employers. Your doctor may prescribe anti-depressants, and these may be necessary, in the short term, to help you through the more traumatic periods.

Seek out self-help groups for mutual support
There are increasing numbers of these types of groups being formed every month. Some are based around a geographic location, whilst others focus on a particular occupation, such as nursing or teaching. Existing support groups throughout the UK are listed in the section Sources of Help and Advice.

You may consider starting one in your area, which will help with the process of regaining control of your life. There are various ways of forming a group, and publicity need not cost anything. Doctors' and dentists' waiting rooms are an excellent source of contacting others with similar interests and concerns. For ideas and guidance on starting a bullying survivor support group, see Tim Field's website successunlimited.

Phone a helpline for advice or support
Services are free and confidential and you may find that speaking to someone who has no intimate knowledge of your *specific* situation can help you to take a more objective view of the problem. For some people, it may be the first time that they have spoken of the situation and the release might be extremely emotional, but extremely beneficial.

However, the fact that many of the people who run the helplines have personal experience of bullying, will help you to know that they understand the effects and implications of the bullying behaviour.

They can also point you to sources of local and national help and support, and a selection of helplines can be found in the resources section.

Investigate personal development groups
If you feel that you could benefit from some support and encouragement to increase your confidence, you may want to attend a local group where this is on offer. Local colleges and universities often run groups at weekends in their continuing education classes. You may get sufficient support from them to give you some strength to tackle the problem. But remember that assertiveness and confidence building is about personal change, and this may be the wrong time for you to tackle this problem without plenty of support.

Helping yourself

Reviewing the situation

Because it is easy to get into a spiral of depression with a feeling of losing control, it is important to try to take a step back from the situation. In these cases try to enlist the help of someone you trust, to assist you in taking an objective view. Although there is a tendency to either avoid thinking of the bullying at all or to become obsessed with the whole thing, you may find 'consciously reflecting' to be useful.

Conscious reflection

Think back to an incident of being bullied and imagine yourself looking down on the situation. At this point you are merely a spectator of this incident and should detach yourself from any relationship you have to the people within it.

Note the various positions of all of the actors in your drama, and what is each one is doing – before, during and after the incident. What words and feelings are now coming to the fore? Is there aggression, manipulation, control, fear, and who is experiencing which of them? What effect is it having on the behaviour of each?

Review your own attitude to the situation. What are your internal thoughts about it? If you are thinking 'Why me?' or 'I can't do anything about it', you will quickly lose the strength to tackle the events.

Try to develop and maintain a positive approach to the situation. Examine the words you use to describe what is happening. If you use words like coping, this gives off a sort of passive acceptance that it can never get any better. Try to use more effective words with an active feel such as handling, tackling, or dealing with. These words are an indication that something is being done by you, and any forward movement, however small, will be a boost to your self-esteem.

Can you now replay the incident, with you directing the action, and making more positive moves? Can you project how you would feel if the situation were resolved? Can this strengthen you to make the first move to tackle it?

Assessing the responsibility

In order to give some context to the situation, assess the responsibilities of all parties in or around the situation. Think about the responsibility you have for your own behaviour and responses. Remember that you do not have responsibility for the behaviour of the bully. You are not 'bringing it on yourself', it isn't your fault. The bully is behaving like they are because they choose to.

What do you see as the organisational responsibility? Are there any policies or procedures that you feel could help you in your situation? An increasing number of organisations are including anti-bullying and harassment policies in their framework and there may be a designated person or procedure that you can tap into.

Even without a specific policy, there is still protection under employment and contract law, which details how organisations should treat their employees and the processes that should be in place to ensure that people are treated fairly.

For some of the more significant ones, see the chapter on legal aspects.

Managing your stress

The insidious thing about negative stress, is that it steadily reduces your will to do anything to tackle it, so that you are sucked into a downward spiral.

Obviously, the more you are feeling stressed, the less motivation you will have to do anything about it. If, however, when you have noticed the effects, you start to take some action to reduce the stress, you will be starting to 'heal' yourself. That will give you the strength to make some decisions on how you tackle the bullying behaviour.

There are many books, videos, tapes and workshops, where you can get information and support regarding management of stress. However, as a first step, and one you can practice immediately, you should be considering the way you breathe.

Effective breathing

One of the most important techniques for managing stress is learning to breathe more efficiently and effectively, and 30 seconds practice every day should help this process:

1 To achieve positive results, your weight should be evenly distributed with feet flat on the floor, whether sitting or standing, and your back as straight as possible.

2 Place one hand on your chest and the other on your abdomen.

3 Breathe slowly, deeply and smoothly through your nose.

4 Consciously pull in your abdomen as you exhale, using your hand to push down your stomach.

5 As you exhale, become aware of your abdominal wall pushing outward.

6 Practice for a few minutes every day so that it becomes your natural pattern or one that you can use as an emergency strategy.

7 You can do this with your eyes open or shut. The decision will, obviously be affected by where you are, but with eyes shut, you become more involved and achieve more benefit from the process.

Tackling the bully

If you have been bullied for some time, or have been subject to intense pressure, the reduction in your confidence levels will obviously be a barrier to confronting the situation and tackling the bullying. You will need to rebuild your confidence even to be able to confront the situation in your own mind and decide how you are going to tackle it.

If you decide to approach the bully yourself, it would be advisable to seek help and support beforehand so that you are able to put your points across assertively and to respond positively to them.

Find out if your organisation has access to a specially trained counsellor, or see if you can approach one yourself outside the workplace.

Investigate assertiveness groups, but this is more of a long-term initiative; a damaged self-confidence will need more than a couple of sessions at an assertiveness workshop.

Read books such as Andrea Adams' *Bullying at Work* (1992), or Tim Field's *Bully in Sight* (1996), which give many examples of how people successfully tackled the bullying. It will help you to see that you are not alone and that the responsibility for the bullying does not belong with you.

Your family or friends can also provide support in building your self-confidence to restore you to a level where you can start to deal with the situation.

> *Aileen received immense support from her elder daughter, Susie, in rebuilding her confidence, after a particularly long and protracted experience of bullying. Susie allowed her mother the space to explore the feeling of low self-esteem and how she now felt totally de-skilled and worthless. Susie helped her mother to compile a list of her skills and attributes, initially taking a long time for Aileen to identify that she had any talents. Starting with the practical skills such as ' cooking', 'able to manage a household budget' etc. she slowly built up the list to include value statements such as 'excellent written*

communication skills', 'popular with work colleagues', 'loving myself'. Through each stage Susie encouraged her mother not only to list these assets, but also to give examples of where she had been able to use them. This ensured that Aileen was not just aimlessly filling up the list, but was able to examine her behaviour and acknowledge that she truly possessed these attributes and skills.

Preparing an initial approach to the bully

If you have recognised the bullying before it has started to affect you too severely and you feel confident enough, you can respond to the bully's behaviour in a way that asserts your right to be treated with respect.

- First, think about whether it is better to speak in private to them or whether you will speak in front of a witness. If the latter, no more than one would be advisable.
- Prepare and practice the statement so that you do not fall over your words. If certain words prove difficult to say, substitute easier ones. Make the sentence or phrase fairly short and make it obvious when you are about to speak and when you are finished. This should prevent the bully being able to manipulate the situation to where you feel less calm and stressed.
- Make the statement when both you and the bully are not under pressure and you have as high a level of confidence as possible. Make sure your blood sugar level is high and that you are not dehydrated.
- Consider your body language at this point. Breathing deeply before and during the challenge, will give you energy and help you maintain a firm and confident stance.
- If you think your hands may shake, hold the back of a chair or the side of a desk in such a way that appears natural.
- Keep your head up and look at the bully directly. Maintaining constant eye contact may be difficult, but ensure that you have their eye when you are putting your point forward and allow your gaze to drop no further than their mouth level when they are responding.
- Say clearly and calmly, that you think their remarks, actions or criticisms are inappropriate and you do not agree with them. Try not to use emotive words such as 'unfair,' 'not right', biased', 'unjust', as these have a value base which could allow the bully to challenge the statement.

Very shortly after Jane, a new personal assistant to the managing director, was appointed, James walked into the office and demanded information which at that time Jane was unable to retrieve. James became abusive, swearing and telling Jane how useless she was. Jane replied in a very calm manner 'I will find the information as soon as I can and I will deliver it to your office. I would ask that you do not come into my office again as I will not have swearing in my office'.

Taking sick leave

If you have taken sick leave because of the stress the bullying is causing you and feel that your employer is trying to force you back to work, write a letter to them, in which you state that your absence is due to stress caused by the inappropriate and negative behaviour of others and this is causing an excessively stressful working environment.

Ask that they fulfil their obligation of duty of care under the Health and Safety at Work Act to provide you with both a safe place of work and a safe system of work.

If you are subsequently victimised for reporting this health and safety hazard, you may find the provisions of the Trade Union Reform and Employment Rights Act 1993 apply, under which tribunals may award substantial compensation.

Invoking the grievance procedure

It may be necessary to invoke your organisation's grievance procedure, although this may be inappropriate and insufficient in a case of bullying, and the organisational culture may support the actions of the bully.

However, if you decide to pursue an action with the Employment Tribunal, it is important that you have shown that you followed all of the options available to you.

Leaving the job

(Based on material from successunlimited).

If the thought of actions involving grievance procedures and employment tribunals is more than you wish to tackle, you may consider leaving your job. This is not an act of failure or weakness, more a positive decision in the face of overwhelming odds which are out of your control and not of your choosing. You have no control over the bully's actions and, alone, you cannot change their behaviour. But you can regain control of your life and take your own decision to leave.

For most people, this will be difficult because of the need for financial security. But you have to decide what is more important, your job or your health?

Making the decision to move on before you are too badly damaged may be the best decision you ever made. By finding an employer who values you and your skills, you can regain your confidence and self-esteem and use the experience to strengthen your resolve never to allow anyone to behave towards you again in a similar manner.

> *I would say that by mid January, I had obvious signs of depression. I used to be a nurse working on a psychiatric unit for two years, and as I was driving by myself up from Newcastle, knowing I had to go back to work soon, the thought crossed my mind of driving into a field. Not to actually kill myself, but if I could sustain some injuries I would have a good excuse to be off work. By the time I returned, maybe some of the ever growing workload, mainly paperwork that I didn't know what to do with, would have been taken care of and maybe the lines would be quieter by then, so I would be able to start afresh.*
>
> *Fortunately, the voice of reason took over and I just kept on driving with tears flowing. By then I had already taken one day off sick, which I put down to food poisoning!, and I think that drive showed me that something had to be done.*
>
> *So, I made an appointment with my GP, and, although meeting this lady for the first time, as soon as she asked me what she could do for me, I just started sobbing and everything poured out.*
>
> *She was very good, listened and gave me the choice between tablets, anti-depressants probably, or a week off work, with the sick note being officially for the flu. I took the week off and had a good think about everything.*
>
> *The next time the bully did something to me, I resigned.*

Janet worked for ten years as a nursery nurse within a primary school. Within the nursery environment and the school, there was a bullying 'regime'. On walking into the school in the morning one could sense the atmosphere, and immediately know what the mood of the place would be that day. Other members of staff protected themselves against Monica, the line manager, in order not to bring her wrath upon themselves. They kept 'in' with her to ensure that they were not singled out. This stifled any creativity and slowly undermined any confidence that Janet had within the workplace.

All Janet's previous appraisals had been glowing, therefore she couldn't understand the difference in behaviour at work with Monica. She still continued to put 110 per cent into everything and always found fault with her own work, even although she knew she couldn't do any more.

One evening, after school, Janet was asked to 'pop in' to Angela's office where she was greeted by Monica, Angela and Dorothy, the deputy head. They sat in a position with their backs to the door and Janet was asked to sit in a seat facing them, on a lower chair, which effectively blocked access to the door.

They then proceeded to tell Janet that she was moody, bad tempered, that nobody liked working with her, she was not good with the children nor their parents, and that she was indeed very lucky to have the job she had. If she moved to another school she would be treated as a skivvy and she would never get as good a job as she had there.

During this interview, Janet steeled herself not to cry, to be strong, stay calm and not break down in front of them but they then accused her of being hard hearted not to show any emotion. As she was driving home she felt that she did not want to go on, that she really must be a terrible person. Looking back on the incident, she realised she must have been very close to suicide.

The continual bullying and harassment prompted her to eventually seek another position in the education environment within primary schools, which she achieved on her second application.

But Janet could not face being in her present workplace any longer and went to her doctor, who signed her off work with a diagnosis of stress until she took up her new post. She also visited the personnel department of the education department and told them what had been happening. They believed her, because they had previous knowledge of the individuals and knew of the situation.

Janet was told that she would have to bring a grievance on harassment if she wanted something done. This is not what she wanted to do. Literature on 'bullying at work' was given to Janet by the personnel department, which helped her realise that she was not going mad.

In the two years since her departure from that environment, Janet still feels very ill at ease. There are places in town where she would never go for fear of bumping into these individuals. If she has to attend a particular course in her new role she goes fearing that there may be someone attending from her previous position, and she feels physically ill. When asked why she did not leave the position and find something else to get out of the situation, Janet said she felt totally unemployable, not worthy of a job and that nobody would want her skills. Janet has no self value, always doubts her work and goes over the top to please the people where she works at present.

After a short period in her new position she was asked by her supervisor to 'pop in' to the office. She did this with fear and trepidation, feeling ill and totally demoralised. Her supervisor thanked her for the work that she had been doing, valued her efforts, and was most appreciative of all that she was trying to do. Janet asked for this to be put in writing for her own sanity and when asked why replied 'Because the last place I was at was difficult'.

Although Janet's training to be a counsellor helped to rationalise some of the ways she was being treated, it has not alleviated the severe distress and damage she has suffered. She had lived her working life totally on edge, constantly in fear of doing something wrong and the more she feared doing something wrong, the more she was hounded.

Even after all the time that has elapsed, not a day goes by without some part of what happened coming back. It was like banging her head against a brick wall and not realising that it hurt until it stopped, and yet she still waits for that pain to start again.

Janet is very aware of her value but still cannot believe it to be true.

Chapter 2
The Bully

> *We knew when somebody was in for it. She'd come in to the office and look around and you could see that someone was going to get it. Her eyes narrowed and it was like being in the sights of a gun. When she passed over you, you just breathed an immense sigh of relief and kept your head down. You knew you were safe for a day or two.*

In his website, Tim Fields states that:

> *...bullying is an obsessive compulsive behaviour and serial bullies seem unable to survive without a target on to whom they can project their inadequacy and incompetence.*

Just as each target is an individual, with their own characteristics, the same is also true of bullies. There are those who everyone recognises as a bully, as in 'He's the macho manager', 'He likes throwing his weight about', or 'I just keep out of his way.' Then there are the ones who are very specific about to whom they show the bullying side of their nature. They are the ones who often have a charming side and they do just that. They charm others.

If whispers start about the bullying, their supporters, the ones who have fallen under the spell, say, 'But that's impossible, they're wonderful – everyone loves them, they do a great job'. This, obviously, is a great deterrent to the target to make a complaint. In fact, they may start to doubt themselves and think that the fault is on their side. 'If everyone else sees this person as wonderful,' they think, 'perhaps I've got it wrong.'

Who are the bullies?

According to a study published in *Survey: Bullying at Work*, April 1999, the percentage of those who exhibited bullying behaviour were:

- line manager .... 45 per cent
- colleagues .... 22 per cent
- groups of colleagues .... 11 per cent
- senior managers .... 8 per cent

Where the bully is in a position of authority, this allows them the power to abuse and threaten, often without challenge.

But bullying by colleagues comes a pretty close second when we look at the effects on the target. This 'peer bullying' can also create a culture where everyone tries to appease or 'get in with' the bully, so as to divert attention and unpleasantness from themselves. This then causes rifts and divisions in the team, where a climate of mistrust prevails.

> *When I first started in the unit, I couldn't understand what was happening. One day some of them would be 'bosom buddies', telling each other intimate and private things, and the*

next day they were talking behind each others' backs, calling them 'cow' and 'bitch' etc. I soon realised I couldn't trust anyone.

How do bullies select their targets?

Although there is less published evidence on the causes of bullying, than on the effects on the target, it may be noted that there appears to be common motives for the bully to behave as they do. The most significant for the target are:

- **Competence**, or even excellence, in one's job, possibly gaining recognition or awards for achievements. The target may be determined and well-motivated, succeeding in all areas and thus be ready for promotion or salary increases. This may highlight or invite comparison with the bully's own feelings of inadequacy and incompetence simply by being competent.
- **Popularity** with colleagues, customers, clients, etc. may also be the starting point for bullying behaviour. It may seem simplistic to attribute jealousy as a cause for bullying to begin, but evidence from recent studies suggests that popularity is a major characteristic of the target.
- **Challenging** bad practice such as incompetence, malpractice, fraud, illegality, breaches of internal procedure or Health and Safety Regulations etc., instigating or suggesting regulatory actions such as joining trades unions may be sufficient to move the bully to select that person as a target. Intervening or standing up for a colleague who is being bullied may lead to the bully transferring or including their attentions to the challenger.

Types of bullying

Unconscious bullying is where the stress of the moment causes behaviour to deteriorate. The person becomes short-tempered, irritable and may shout or swear at others, but when the pressure is removed, behaviour returns to normal and the person recognises the inappropriateness of their behaviour, makes amends, and probably apologises. Importantly, they learn from the experience so that next time the situation arises they are better able to deal with it. The most significant factor in this is its short term and temporary nature, unlike conscious bullying, which is defined by its motivation to humiliate and damage.

Corporate bullying is where the culture is one of fear and blame. Knowing that the law is inadequate and jobs are scarce, an employer can abuse, or allow employees to be abused, with impunity. This can promote learned behaviour, where employees who have been bullied or who have witnessed bullying, use that as their model of behaviour and may, in turn, bully others.

After leaving university, Michael had joined his family's manufacturing firm as a junior member of staff. His line manager, and subsequently his head of unit, ran the department by bullying. He constantly humiliated and berated staff for every mistake, real or imagined. The Monday morning planning meetings became a battleground where everyone kept their head down to avoid drawing attention to themselves. When the bully had picked their target for the day, a feeling of relief was palpable and the others would isolate the target out of self-preservation. Many extremely talented and skilled people left the company rather than suffer the constant humiliation of the bully's behaviour.

As Michael rose through the ranks to take over the company, his style of 'management' was embedded in a blame culture. Staff were reluctant to take any chances in developing or trying innovative approaches to the market, for fear of attracting his attention. Just as his role model had done before, Michael was losing the brightest and the best to other companies.

Serial bullying is where one individual, picks on one employee after another and damages them. Tim Fields, in his website, successunlimited, notes that this is the most common type of bullying and the one most people are familiar with, (see the case of Alan).

Group bullying. Sometimes, the bully joins with others and may bully as a pair or as part of a group. Occasionally, the bully has willing associates, but in other cases people join in with the bullying to stop it happening to them. This form of bullying takes on other forms of intimidation, with the group becoming a mob.

Amanda had trouble with one of her colleagues who consistently belittled any contribution she had made in meetings. He persistently criticised her reports in public and lost no opportunity to sneer at every effort she made. Amanda was a confident person and felt that she could handle this constant sniping, even though it was taking a great deal out of her. Finally, at the Christmas party, the bully led a chant against her, encouraging all of her colleagues to join in. 'That,' said Amanda, ' was the final straw. I just broke down and became almost uncontrollable. All of the pressure I thought I was coping with, just piled on top of me. By getting my colleagues to gang up on me, he completely destroyed my strength and my confidence in myself. I left the office and I have never returned.

Calum was newly into teaching and was rather shocked when confronted by two female colleagues who appeared to take great delight in taunting him about his lack of experience. He heard them making fun of him in front of some of the pupils, which made it difficult to maintain any order in the classroom. A common tactic was that the pair always seemed to be around whenever he tried to gain access to the computer and they would insist that it was unavailable, as they had booked it previously. They also made a point of standing very close to him, face to face. This made him feel extremely uncomfortable, but also nervous of moving towards them in case they claimed sexual harassment.

Organisational bullying is a combination of pressure bullying and corporate bullying, and occurs when an organisation struggles to adapt to changing priorities, reduced funding, cuts in budgets, imposed expectations, and other external pressures. Some results of this situation might be:

- Where employees are made to work 60, 70 or even 80 hour weeks on a regular basis, and anyone who objects finds life is made very uncomfortable for them, or they are even dismissed.
- When employees suffering from stress are castigated as being weak and inadequate, and those who look like having a stress breakdown are dismissed.
- Where 'absence management' is introduced to deny employees annual or sick leave to which they are genuinely entitled.
- By using 'micro-management', such as regularly checking up on employees, e.g. by listening in to telephone conversations, and asking leading questions of colleagues.
- Having an open door for employees, to encourage others to fabricate complaints about colleagues.

Bullying by subordinates. Bullying can also occur where managers and supervisors are bullied either by subordinate individuals, or groups, although group bullying is more common. In this form the bullying is directed upwards to make the supervisor feel useless and out of control. This form of bullying is often found when a newly recruited or promoted manager is put in charge of a stable and strong group of workers. Because they have little experience, the manager may rely on part of the workforce to enforce some of the discipline. Unfortunately, this can be at the expense of the target's own authority. The group may gossip about them, sowing seeds of doubt and suspicion in the minds of others, or they may simply refuse to co-operate and follow instructions, making the target look and feel as if they are doing the bullying.

Selecting the target

The selection of a particular target is mentioned by many who have experienced or witnessed bullying. Sometimes, it's almost a case of everyone 'taking a turn' at being the target. In others, the bully focuses their attention on one person until they have finished with them, often because they have gone off sick, have left work – or worse, and then turns to another target.

> *Alan was a branch manager of a large financial organisation and had come late into this type of business. However, he proved to be an excellent worker and his promotion to manager was a popular move. In his early days, he remembers witnessing the bullying behaviour of the Chief Executive towards a colleague and this colleague's gradual decline of confidence until the point that he left work and eventually committed suicide.*
>
> *'Within days of this person leaving, I realised that the Chief Executive had transferred his attentions to me. Suddenly, I wasn't doing anything right. He challenged my every decision. Investigations into my performance were carried out and I passed every one with flying colours. But this still did not satisfy this man. In one day he sent me 42 memos detailing trivial complaints about my work.'*

Bullying or management?

Bullying is a systematic behaviour rather than one that is erratic, inexperienced or unskilled and, although this erratic behaviour is often difficult to deal with at the time, it may be worked around. Especially if, in moments of calm and logic, the person is open to comment and discussion about their behaviour. The *intent* to humiliate and destroy confidence is not a feature of this particular behaviour as it is with the bully.

Another aspect of bullying is the frequency and intensity of the behaviour. It may also include unpredictability, like changing the goalposts or priorities without warning or even informing, and constant inappropriate comment, such as belittling a person's physical appearance.

Damaging the organisation

Undoubtedly, the damage that the bully does to the target will have far reaching implications to the individual. But the amount of damage that a bully does to the organisation is possibly not fully acknowledged by a management who may prefer to ignore these matters. A bully who is spending time persecuting a worker, such as in Alan's case, is spending far more time on that agenda than in the pursuance of organisational goals. The composition of 42 memos, allowing even just five minutes for each, would result in three and a half hours of wasted and unproductive time, around 50 per cent of the working day!

Forms of bullying

Bullying has many forms and some or all of the list below may be present. However, this list is very far from being exhaustive and new and more insidious ways are constantly being utilised.

For example, the growing use of e-mail within and between offices, is proving to be another medium for the bully to create fear and uncertainty. Others are:

- Excessive supervision.
- Excessive and unwarranted criticism.
- Setting impossible goals and performance levels.
- Constantly humiliating or ridiculing.
- Isolating the target from the rest of the workforce.
- Constantly changing goals and priorities.
- Withholding vital information.
- Abusive or offensive personal remarks.
- Consistently undervaluing or devaluing work.
- Imposing inappropriate work sanctions.

Just talking about it now, I realise I have gone from the frying pan into the fire. My current boss is a bully; I guess I knew it all along subconsciously, but didn't want to face the problem all over again. Luckily, this time the bully doesn't use just me as the target but bullies everyone in the department. He fits just about every single one of the categories.

So what makes a bully?

Although studies have been carried out on the effects of bullying, there has been little research into what makes a person bully others.

At times, bullying behaviour may be seen in any of us, with the pressure to perform, deliver the goods, or meet the targets. If we have responsibility for others and their work performance, we can be pushed into unreasonable behaviour and maybe behave out of character.

But the key difference between management and 'performance anxiety' and bullying is that bullying can be seen as 'The continual and relentless attack on other people's self-confidence and self esteem in an intentional, regular and repeated manner'.

Bullying by management often occurs when managers are untrained in the proper skills of motivation and leadership.

As Lisa recalls:

> *Amed started off at the company as a computer programmer. He was hopeless and was shifted around departments until he couldn't be shifted around anymore. He then spent time brown-nosing the then manager. From all accounts he is a Jekyll and Hyde character and behaves totally differently with the MD of the company.*

Why do people bully?

- The bully is envious of another person's social standing or professional ability.
- They bully those they consider to be a threat to their own position.
- They are bullied themselves and 'pass the parcel'.
- They think bullying is the best way to make other people work harder.
- They start to bully after 'being nice' fails to get the required results.
- They bully sadistically, for their own pleasure.
- They want to push staff into resigning.
- They want to give themselves a 'macho' image.

Bullying characteristics

Insecurity: It has been said that bullies are also cowards. As the psychology of bullying is based on insecurity the typical bully may feel inadequate or insecure and bullies others to compensate for these perceived shortcomings. The bully may then project their own faults onto the target.

The Jekyll and Hyde character: One aspect that is reported by people experiencing or witnessing bullying, is that bullies often show one face to the target while appearing charming to others. This compounds the problem for the target who may find it difficult to convince others that they are being bullied.

Over-sensitivity to criticism: The bully may dislike being shown to be wrong and may try to blame the target on their mistakes or rearrange responsibilities so that the target is set up to fail and thus take responsibility for the bully's action.

Dishonesty: Bullies are often devious people who like to disguise their behaviour either to themselves or to others.

Based on the work of Ruth Wheatley.

Psychology of the bully

Bullying in adulthood can be the result of being bullied in childhood, either by an adult or an older child. As they grow up, they may identify with the dominant aggressor's role and take on the behaviour and attitudes to which they themselves were subjected.

Bullies often feel a need to show strength, probably as a reaction to a childhood where they felt themselves to be weak. The bully then says, subconsciously, to themselves:

'This time I will be the one who wins; I am the one who is in control and determines the outcome'.

Alternatively, as children they may have been brought up by their parents to believe that they are the centre of the universe and that everything revolves around them. They cannot see that their behaviour is their own responsibility, but believe that other people cause their problems.

Bullies are often frightened of being 'found out', and so by terrorising other people and keeping them at arms' length, they cannot be discovered or exposed as being weak.

Bullying often comes from envy. They resent and envy those people who they feel are competent and able at their jobs. They feel threatened and need to bring the target down to a level the bully can deal with and not feel threatened by. Also, by bullying, they are able to rob the targets of their feeling of pleasure at doing a job well.

Bullies may feel threatened by a colleague's or subordinate's success and bullies to keep them 'in their place'. They may be in a special or privileged position in a company and want to make sure they are not supplanted by the target.

> *I did realise at one point that this particular person was probably very insecure, and her main 'work' knowledge was based on routine that she gained by working there from day one on. Often, when asked for help, she didn't have time or you were told that you should know this by now.*
>
> *When looking closer, in terms of product pricing for example, I noticed that some of the other colleagues knew them, while she had to look them up.*
>
> *I even suspect that maybe in her subconscious she could never bear to have 'equal' colleagues. She was carving out this little power niche for herself and of course being invaluable to the company by being one of the very few who really knew the ropes and maintaining this status by getting rid of new staff, she is the wonderful person, who is oh so committed.*

> *The power behind envy bullying lies in its subtle slights that hurt the recipient but can be disguised from onlookers. The message to the target is 'You are not worthy. You are being sidelined'.*
>
> Andrea Adams (1992)

Often the bully makes the target feel small and insignificant and so that the target feels as if their own outrage is irrational. By making the target feel as if it is they who have a problem, the bully is able to delude themselves that it is not connected with themselves in any way.

> *Those subjected to aggression not only feel victims of it, but are also made to doubt their own perception of events.*
>
> Andrea Adams (1992)

Bullies may also create a working environment whereby certain people are favourites and are invited to the 'inner circle' and then are dropped for no reason. This results in an atmosphere of uncertainty and confusion in which people try harder to win back the bully's affections and attention. The bully may surround themselves with willing partners, and if the target does not conform to that pattern, they will forever be on the outside. Sometimes, a potential target will join this mob rather than suffer the isolation, even when this means joining with the bully and watching as they terrorise another target.

Adapted from the work of Ruth Wheatley.

Psychological tactics

Bullies may use the following psychological tactics to intimidate the target:

- **Aggression:** This feeds on humiliation and embarrassment. The bully may be unaware that they are behaving in this way and believe that they are simply exhibiting 'strong management'. However, this is a classic behaviour to keep people 'in their place' by exhibiting aggressive tendencies. Most people will give in rather than face confrontation, and this suits the bully since subjugation is the aim.
- **Dominance:** The bully must keep the target at arms' length. To let the target close is to let them realise that the bully is insecure and frightened, and they feel that if people get too close, they will be able to see through them.
- **Guilt:** The bully makes the target feel guilty for something that they have or haven't done. Punishment for some perceived transgression may be the withdrawal of affection or privileges. This is a very powerful issue in voluntary sector bullying, where the target is often made to feel guilty by asking for rights like time off for doctor appointments or even wanting to leave work at the correct time at the end of the day.
- **Power:** As knowledge is power, the bullies may keep useful information to themselves, thus making it impossible for the target to do a good job. The bully may also be unwilling, or unable, to delegate but simply dumps work on their subordinates.
- **Threats:** The bully may use threats to subjugate and control the target and others around the workplace. These can be minor sanctions or the ultimate one of sacking.

Based on the work of Ruth Wheatley.

Brian was a man who got the job done. His bosses knew they could rely on him to get results and they didn't enquire too closely into his methods. His work was his life and the long hours he worked had cost him his marriage. His social life was also non-existent due to his manner of sneering at people's efforts and always trying to take over everything he was involved in.

When he became a manager, he knew that he could put right all the slacking and 'skiving' that he felt went on in the department.

He soon noticed that not everyone seemed as committed as himself to working overtime or coming in on a Saturday. He started to become increasingly annoyed at hearing about people's plans for the weekend or hearing what they'd done the previous evening. One of the team, Andrew, had an especially busy social life, being a member of a drama group and a choir. He also seemed to have a very stable and happy marriage.

Brian resented this and took every opportunity to belittle Andrew's work, returning reports with red pen marks on trivial mistakes, and often inventing reasons for rejecting the work.

Andrew tried harder and harder to meet these standards that Brian was imposing, but to no avail. The motive was not improvement, but control and humiliation.

Eventually, Andrew complained to the personnel manager, who interviewed Brian, but he denied bullying. He commented that Andrew was just lazy, more concerned with going out and having a good time than doing a proper day's work. Because it was one word against another with no witnesses and no evidence, and because Brian did get results, personnel took his word and Andrew was subject to the disciplinary procedure. Eventually, Andrew realised it wasn't going to get any better and so he left the company.

Once his target had gone, Brian waited for a period of three days, a new target was selected and the process started all over again.

This, then, happened twice more, before Brian's employers realised that the targets had been telling the truth. Now they felt threatened, as they realised that they might have sided with the wrong person in the past. But to admit that mistake might have incurred liability if legal action were taken. So they offered Peter, the latest target to complain, a small out-of-court settlement with a comprehensive gagging clause.

Brian is still a manager with the company.

Are you a bully?

Now that you have become familiar with the characteristics and actions of the bully, can you see yourself in any of them?

- Is yours a workplace where people are secondary to the work in hand?
- Is the culture one of blame and fault-finding, with everyone trying to meet impossible goals with little or no support and resources?
- Have there been significant changes in the composition or intensity of your workload?

Are you:

- Giving other people impossible targets to meet?
- Refusing reasonable requests for leave?
- Using sarcasm or humiliation as a way of managing people?
- Picking out small faults, while ignoring overall good performances?

Do you:

- Single people out for criticism?
- Believe that people work better when they feel their jobs are in danger?
- Exclude people from meetings?
- Withhold information from people?
- Shout at people?
- Change guidelines or procedures without consultation?
- Treat different people differently?

Based on the work of Ruth Wheatley.

Chapter 3
The Manager

Management is the co-ordination and allocation of resources in a supportive and motivational environment, encouraging personnel to perform and develop work-based tasks within the remit of organisational goals.

As with many things, the style of management in any organisation will be influenced by factors such as the culture, the current operational procedures and often by reactive factors such as crisis and expediency.

Changes to the role

Over the past few years there has been a marked shift in the role of the manager from being directive to being collaborative. For some managers, this has been a welcome change and one into which they fit comfortably.

However, this collaborative approach and a move towards flatter organisational structures can be a source of stress. Adding these new workplace approaches to a situation where lack of finance and an increase in targets is becoming the norm, managers can find themselves being pressured to raise performance levels to almost unattainable heights, with decreasing resources and personnel.

Whilst the manager is without support to fulfil these goals, they can find themselves operating in a way that promotes a negative culture. In these situations, the potential for bullying becomes very real.

Within one factory, a particular manager, James, was very vociferous when it came to wanting things done. His language was dreadful, and he would continually swear when things weren't going his way. Even when he dealt with suppliers of the company, he would swear at them and could be heard by people well outside his own office. He treated his staff very badly, yet none of them complained. They all worked excessive amounts of overtime, not leaving until James did, as he expected them to be there. James never took time off work – with colds, feeling unwell or even when he broke his leg – he always came in to work. He expected his staff to be the same. If any staff were off sick he would phone to ask about a particular job being done. On one occasion there was no answer, so he sent the company car round to find out where the person was.

Skills required by managers

- Act as positive role model to your staff.
- Be an active listener.
- Take the lead in new ventures.
- Show yourself to be open to feedback and criticism.

- Be willing to learn and adapt to changes.
- Be ambitious for the future of the organisation.
- Use facilitation rather than direction.
- Project a collaborative image.

Supporting the target

If you are a manager or supervisor and are approached for advice or support in a case of bullying:

- **Create a comfortable atmosphere:** Obviously this will need to be in private and somewhere where you will not be disturbed. Make it clear that you are prepared to take time to deal with the problem. If you are not available at that time, make a specific time commitment to deal with it. The tone of your voice and a sympathetic eye contact will show a willingness to listen.

- **Take the situation seriously:** Be aware of the tension in the situation and attempt to defuse it – without denying the impact it is having on both of you. Avoid the temptation to rush in and offer solutions; or to make conciliatory statements such as, 'Well, it's just their way, I'm sure they didn't mean it'.

- **Listen for the real problem:** The intensity of the emotions felt by people being bullied may prevent them from being rational and clear about the problem. They may not even know what is the cause of the problem, and only be aware of the impact on themselves, their work and their general behaviour. In cases of long-term bullying, a person may find it difficult to express themselves logically and objectively.

- **Listen more than you speak:** Don't question them intently or ask anything that might make them feel that they have done something wrong. When they start to talk, listen carefully to what they have to say. Once they begin to discuss the bullying, it may seem to be all they can talk about, and even if the person seems to be making wild generalisations, allow them space to clarify their statements. Be patient and let them go on, it's better for them to let it all out than to bottle it up.

- **Be prepared to hear criticisms:** These may not be just about the bully. For instance, if the target feels that one of the ways they are being bullied is by being set unrealistic or constantly changing goals, this may have implications about the overall way of goal setting in the unit or department. It is important at this point not to become defensive about the system, but to continue to listen actively and neutrally.

- **Remember your impartiality:** If you are to operate in an atmosphere of openness and equality, it is important to listen to the full story and give everyone in the situation a chance to make their views heard.

- **Keep up-to-date:** If, as a manager, you want to support your staff, you will need to be aware of current policies and keep up-to-date with revisions and amendments. Find out the names of current support staff and contact them before a problem arises to confirm the procedures. Keep copies of any literature regarding the appropriate policies in your office, so that you can produce them when necessary. This will indicate to your staff that you take the procedures seriously. This can support a potential target and discourage a potential bully.

Differences between managing and bullying

The Manager:	The Bully:
• uses power carefully	• abuses their power over others
• respects confidentiality	• has no respect for confidentiality
• values people's contributions	• devalues or ignores people's contributions
• encourages innovation and creativity	• stifles innovation and creativity
• instills trust in their staff	• engenders mistrust in their staff
• respects the individual	• has no respect for anyone
• utilises skills for the common good	• uses people's skills for their own ends
• encourages self-development	• discourages all development
• rewards people's efforts	• ignores people's efforts
• supports staff in times of concern	• has no concern for staff at any time
• accepts the occasional weakness	• sees weakness as unacceptable
• accepts that humans make mistakes	• punishes people for mistakes
• listens to staff concerns and acts on them	• ignores staff concerns
• encourages team work	• likes to isolate individuals
• motivates inexperienced staff	• ridicules inexperienced staff
• rejoices in people's successes	• is envious of others' successes
• respects people's personal space	• intrudes in personal space
• looks for solutions to problems	• looks to blame
• plans ahead	• exercises little vision
• is a forward thinker	• is a reactive thinker
• encourages and fosters change	• is frightened of change
• is able to accept criticism	• rejects all criticism
• works towards organisational goals	• works to their own agenda

Chapter 4
Blowing the Whistle

Definition

The unauthorised disclosure of information that an employee reasonably believes is evidence of the contravention of any law, rule or regulation, code of practice or professional statement, that involves mis-management, corruption, abuse of authority or danger to public or worker health and safety.

(Vinten, 1994)

'Blowing the whistle'

In some circumstances, people may feel that they are being bullied because they have attempted to alert someone in authority to a misdemeanour, cover-up, malpractice or other act that is either morally or legally wrong.

Since the Public Interest Disclosure Act 1998 came into force on 2nd July 1999, there are now prescribed means for the malpractice to be reported and also to protect the 'whistleblower'.

The Act applies to every factory, hospital, Whitehall department, charity, office, shop and QUANGO in the UK and covers employees who raise concerns about:

- The maltreatment of patients.
- Financial mismanagement.
- Health and safety in the workplace.
- Consumer protection.
- Regulatory non-compliance.
- Breaches of contract.
- Cover-ups and crimes committed at work.
- Miscarriages of justice.
- Breaches of civil service code.
- Abuse in care.
- Risks to the environment.
- Cover-ups of questionable practice.

Accountability

The Act promotes accountability in all sectors and encourages people to come forward about malpractice in the workplace.

The Act ensures that organisations deal with the message and not the messenger and lessens the temptation for organisations to cover up serious acts of malpractice.

Protection

The Act protects workers against acts of reprisal by their employer, that is, denial of promotion, facilities or training opportunities which would otherwise have been available.

The workers who are covered include:

- persons who work under contracts of employment
- persons who work under personal contract
- homeworkers
- certain agency workers
- certain dentists and pharmacists
- certain categories of trainee

Workers not covered include those who are:

- self-employed
- in the intelligence services
- in the army
- in the police service

The Act protects public interest disclosures to regulators, the media and MPs and workers may make a claim for unfair dismissal if they are dismissed for making a protected disclosure.

Protected disclosures

Certain categories of claim are the subject of special protection. The disclosure must have at least one or more of the following:

- That a criminal offence has been committed or is likely to be committed.
- That a person has failed, or is likely to fail, to comply with any legal obligations to which they are subject.
- That a miscarriage of justice has occurred, is occurring or is likely to occur.
- That health or safety has been, or is likely to be, endangered.
- That the environment has been, is being, or is likely to be damaged.
- That information tending to show any matter falling within any one of the preceding paragraphs has been, is being or is likely to be deliberately concealed.

It is not necessary to prove that a criminal act has been committed. The whistleblower has only to have a reasonable belief that this is so.

It should be noted that the person making the disclosure commits an offence by making the allegation if the action is protected by the Official Secrets Act or that legal professional privilege would apply.

The disclosure must be made in one of the following ways:

- To an employer or another person who is responsible for the matter disclosed.
- To a legal adviser.
- To a Minister of the Crown.
- To a 'prescribed person'.
- It is made in 'other cases'.
- It is an 'exceptionally serious' breach.

'Prescribed person'

If the employee is concerned about a wrongdoing they can make disclosures to a body or a person who is authorised by the Secretary of State to receive disclosures about the matter concerned. The disclosure will be protected, provided the worker:

- Makes the disclosure in good faith.
- Reasonably believes that the allegation is substantially true.
- Reasonably believes that the matter falls within the description of matters for which the body or person has been prescribed.

'Reasonable' must take into account:

- The identity of the person or body to whom the allegation is made.
- The seriousness of the alleged failure.
- Whether or not the relevant failure has continued or is likely to continue.
- The action a person, to whom a previous disclosure was made or might have been made, has taken (or might reasonably be expected to have taken, as a result of a previous disclosure).
- Whether in making the disclosure to the employer the worker complied with any procedure whose use by them was authorised by the employer.

'Other cases'

Disclosure is protected providing:

- At the time of the disclosure, the whistleblower reasonably believes that they will be treated detrimentally by their employer if the allegation is made to them.
- That the employee reasonably believes that evidence relating to the action will be concealed or destroyed if they make the disclosure to their employer.
- The worker has previously disclosed information of substantially the same nature to their employer or a 'prescribed person' or body.

'Exceptionally serious' breaches

These relate to a situation in which the disclosure is serious enough to merit bypassing the other procedures. The worker must show that:

- The disclosure was made in good faith.
- The writer believes that the allegation and information are substantially true.
- The allegation is of an exceptionally serious nature.
- Given the circumstances, it is reasonable to make the disclosure.

Unfair dismissal

The employee who has been dismissed as the result of making a disclosure must make a claim for unfair dismissal within three months of dismissal. The one-year qualifying period for unfair dismissal does not apply in cases of protected disclosures.

Compensation

The Public Disclosure (Compensation) Regulations 1999 modify the provisions of the Employment Rights Act 1996 relating to compensation as a result of protected disclosure. The Regulations remove the monetary limit on the amount of compensation. The award is to be compensatory rather than punitive and is determined by the whistleblower's loss.

Tribunal's considerations

If the 'reasonableness' conditions of whistleblowing are met, the tribunal hearing the case will then consider the identity of the person or body to whom the disclosure was made. It will also consider the gravity of the allegation, whether or not the danger or malpractice remains and whether or not it breached a duty of confidence owed to a third party. If the disclosure was made to the employer or prescribed regulator, the tribunal will also take into consideration that person's or body's response to the allegations.

The whistleblower's considerations

If you are considering 'blowing the whistle' on your employer or another body, it is worth going through the following steps first:

- Talk to your family or close friends about your decision to make the allegations.
- Discreetly find out if anyone else knows about the malpractices and if they have also taken steps to address this.
- Investigate ways of dealing with the problem within the organisation before 'breaking ranks'.
- If you decide to pursue the allegations, decide if you want to give your name or make the allegations anonymously.
- Develop a plan for when and to whom to make the allegations.
- Keep a careful record of events before and after you make the allegations of wrongdoing.
- Make and keep copies of all supporting evidence.
- Contact a solicitor.
- Make the allegations in your own time, not your employer's.

Possible repercussions

Institutions and organisations may use actions that diminish the power of the whistle-blower in ways that resemble bullying or harassment. These actions may include:

- stonewalling
- evasion
- denying the reality of the situation
- isolating and freezing out the individual
- changing work schedules
- closing ranks
- spying on the individual
- cosmetically reshuffling the organisation

The realities of whistleblowing

- Be sure that the allegations are true miscarriages of justice rather than merely questionable business practice.
- Find out about the potential damage your allegations may cause to your:
  - organisation
  - colleagues
  - family
  - shareholders
  - clients
  - students
  - patients
- Familiarise yourself with the relevant legislation.
- Exhaust all internal channels first.
- Enlist the support of other people in the organisation.
- Approach someone higher up in the organisation to act as a sounding board.
- Continue working hard, staying focussed, and keep the lines of communication open with your employer.
- Keep yourself informed of employment rights by contacting a solicitor.
- Consider your options:
  - resign and go public with your allegations
  - stay and make the allegations anonymously
  - stay and make the allegations publicly
  - stay and say nothing
  - take your complaint to the relevant body or person

Further information

The list of 30 prescribed persons and bodies is published in Supplement 28 of the *Employment Contracts Handbook*.

Section 2

The Organisational Perspective

Chapter 5
Assessing the Situation

Bullying is more than a firm management style: it is destructive rather than constructive. It is criticism of a person rather than their mistakes and publicly humiliates them rather than privately corrects. It can result in an individual feeling threatened or compromised.

Bullying usually results from a mis-use of authority within an organisation. It can also result from a mis-use of any form of individual power: such as physical strength, personality or age: or collective power through strength of numbers.

(Introduction to Guidelines Relating to Dignity at Work Policy, Fife Council, 1997)

Bullying can happen in organisations of all types, large and small, in the private and not-for-profit sectors. This behaviour impacts not only on the target but also on those witnessing it and, ultimately, on the organisation. Even when the bullying is not visible, the result of allowing the bullying to happen is reflected in higher operating costs, reduced productivity and probably the loss of key personnel.

Recognising the potential for bullying

Recent research by bodies such as The Institute of Personnel and Development and Staffordshire University Business School has found that a majority of people experience bullying in their workplace, either as the target or as a witness to the bullying behaviour.

The research has also suggested that certain environmental conditions and organisational structures can actually encourage bullying behaviour and a bullying culture.

The Manufacturing, Science and Finance Union guidance suggests that an organisation may accidentally or deliberately encourage bullies through cultures that result in:

- a fear for one's position
- an authoritarian style of supervision
- frequent organisational change and uncertainty
- little participation
- lack of training
- poor working relationships
- excessive workloads
- no clear codes of acceptable conduct
- no procedures for resolving problems

General factors

- New employees are denied basic information about the systems etc., either through lack of time being made available for appropriate induction procedures or as a deliberate attempt to keep employees 'in the dark' about their rights.
- Line managers are not coping with existing workloads.
- There is a mismatch of expectations.
- Job descriptions are vague or dishonest or do not identify the boundaries or scope of the workload.
- Unattainable targets are set.
- There is ignorance about protective policies, grievance and disciplinary procedures, the law etc.

Specific factors affecting schools

- Regular inspections.
- Increased competition between schools to attract pupils.
- 'Marketplace philosophies' imposed on the management structure.
- Extra administration and business techniques becoming part of the workload.
- Extra stress on managers and head teachers, who in turn pressurise their subordinates, causing a knock-on effect, or 'cascade bullying.'

In addition, sick and pregnant teachers are often identified as targets as there is often a lack of money to cover for absent staff. Those who have been bullied, or witnessed bullying, say their reasons for keeping silent about it included job insecurity and fear of adverse publicity, which might attract fewer pupils and jeopardise their own and others' jobs.

Specific factors affecting voluntary organisations

- Lack of job security due to short or fixed term contracts.
- Increased pressure on managers to achieve objectives, often with a reduced work force or budget.
- Absence of policies to formally highlight and address concerns.
- Absence of procedures for resolving interpersonal issues and conflict.
- Lack of training in management, supervisory or interpersonal skills.
- No effective line management and support structure.
- The management committee or board members have minimal experience or time available to give to being an effective employer.

Assessing the costs

The visible costs

- **£485** per employee on average for annual sickness absence (HSE).
- **£5,000** minimum in recruitment costs to replace one employee, plus the reduced performance whilst they are getting to grips with the job.

- **£7 billion** cumulative annual cost to industry, The National Health Service and taxpayers, (Institute of Management Report, 1996).
- **£5 billion** (TUC) to **£12 billion** (CBI) annual estimates of the cost of stress-related illness to business and The National Health Service, which means that's £500 for every working adult.

The hidden costs

Bullies in the workforce are a significant factor in reducing profitability or affecting viability because:

- The bully is not managing their staff, time or resources effectively, but still draws a full salary. Private agendas, not organisational objectives, are being pursued.
- The target becomes demotivated and, through fear, can start to under-perform, which leads to increasing sick leave being taken.
- Other staff feel the effect of the bully's behaviour and spend increasing amounts of time covering their backs and keeping a low profile, thereby reducing the amount of effective work carried out. There is a reduction in creative and innovative work as the bully's unpredictability will affect people's risk-taking.

In addition, results from recent studies undertaken on this issue state:

- Six million working days are lost annually due to stress caused by bullying, job insecurity, shift work and long hours (HSE).
- One in eight, or around three million UK employees have been bullied at work in the last five years. (IPD).
- Estimates show that up to 50 per cent of all stress-related illnesses are caused by bullying. (UMIST).
- One in three people leave their job as a result of being bullied.

Non-financial costs

Those working in voluntary and not-for-profit sectors may find it difficult to assess the damaging implications on an organisation without the bottom line of reduced profits and performance. But the high cost of recruitment and training new members of staff is a significant drain on the limited amounts of money available to finance the project or organisation.

The non-financial aspects can be easily identified when looking at the levels of morale and motivation present, the amount of innovative and development work happening and the general atmosphere in the workplace.

Assessing the responsibilities

Although there is a need for people to take responsibility for their own behaviour, organisations have a statutory duty to ensure that the workplace is a safe environment.

The Health and Safety at Work Act 1974 requires, 'an employer to take reasonable practical measures to ensure the health, safety and welfare of its employers and others sharing the workplace.'

Management of Health and Safety at Work Regulations

These require an employer to ensure the health and safety of employees and others affected by their work activities, and conduct assessments of the risks to which employees are exposed. Employers who fail to take reasonable steps to protect the health and safety of their employees are subject to action through the courts by the Health and Safety Executive (HSE).

Although very few prosecutions have occurred, it is interesting to note that the HSE now acknowledge the part played by bullying by including it as a significant cause of stress in their guidelines, *Stress at Work*, (1995).

A recent report by the HSE also highlighted the causes of work-related illnesses:

- 55 per cent caused by excessive workloads or pace of work
- 26 per cent due to lack of managerial support
- 11 per cent by conflict with members of the public
- 10 per cent from relationships at work, including bullying and harassment

Duty of care

The organisational responsibility of employers, managers, human resource professionals etc. in tackling the problem of workplace bullying, cannot be underestimated.

Croner's *A-Z Guide to Managing People* states that employers may be potentially liable for stress caused to employees where they have negligently placed that employee's health at risk, and that the employee could have grounds for a personal injury claim. However, for a claim to succeed, there must be certain conditions present:

- The employer must owe the employee a duty of care.
- The employer must be in breach of that duty.
- The employee must suffer an injury.
- The employer's breach must have caused that injury.
- It must have been reasonably foreseeable.

The case of *Walker v Northumberland County Council* established that the risk of mental damage, due for example to stress, could now be included in the duty of care.

In the case of *Ballantyne v South Lanarkshire Council*, a social worker who was forced into early retirement because of the 'outspoken' and 'abusive' behaviour of her boss, won £66,000 in an out-of-court settlement. South Lanarkshire Council conceded the case, admitting that there had been shortcomings in how this member was managed.

Chapter 6
Taking Action

Creating an anti-bullying environment

Creating an anti-bullying environment is a comprehensive and challenging objective, which needs to be carefully thought through before you start any implementation of the procedures.

Like all culture changes, this needs to come with a commitment from the top management. Without the authority for the utilisation of extra resources and a major change in policies and procedures, this initiative has little chance of succeeding. Because this initiative is about a major organisational culture change, it is important to set realistic goals. Factors such as the degree of resistance and the sheer mechanics of communications will significantly influence the time required for change to be achieved.

Organisations that are already implementing well-designed procedures such as 'equal opportunities' or 'working with diversity' will be further into the culture where respect for people is part of the organisational life. These organisations and ones with only a few employees could expect to complete the transition inside a year.

In organisations where there is no existing framework of people-oriented policies and procedures or in those where bullying and harassment is a way of working, it may be more realistic to plan for around two years.

Your plan will probably contain the following elements:

- Acknowledging the existence of bullying and the possibility that it is happening in your organisation.
- Making the commitment to identify the causes and the scope of the problem.
- Taking steps to identify and communicate the effects and implications of the issue.
- Developing a 'Positive Culture' or 'Dignity at Work' initiative, based on the development of relevant policies to address the various issues that you have identified.
- Creating effective procedures and structures, which enable individuals to address the issues.
- Putting in place effective monitoring and evaluation processes.

Acknowledging the issue

It is vital that everyone is involved from the start and can contribute to the process. To ensure that this is communicated to all staff, volunteers, committee members, trustees, and so on, it will be useful to publish a 'Statement of Intent', (see Figure 2) to prepare everyone for the change.

This statement also gives people the opportunity to comment on, and be part of, the process.

Figure 2

Name of Organisation: ....

Statement of intent
We are, as an organisation, committed to eliminating all forms of inappropriate behaviour including harassment, bullying and victimisation.

We believe that such behaviour undermines the dignity of all of those affected and we have determined that it will not be tolerated.

We further believe that all individuals have a right to be treated with dignity and respect whilst at work, or where it has an effect on work.

This initiative is central to the aims and values of this organisation and, in particular, it emphasises equality and quality in an open and accountable workplace where employees are supported and valued.

The aim of this organisation is to provide a constructive, positive workplace and a supportive working environment free from offensive behaviour.

This initiative is intended to prevent all forms of offensive behaviour, whether or not such behaviour is deemed to be unlawful.

All formal complaints made within the scope of this initiative will be fairly investigated and may result in disciplinary proceedings, and managers have a duty to implement all procedures arising from this initiative and to ensure that all employees are treated with dignity and respect.

Guidelines for managers and employees will be drawn up to facilitate the implementation of this initiative and to ensure a maximum level of consistency.

These guidelines will be published throughout the organisation and the contents made known to all new and existing employees.

All employees and those people who are involved in the work of this organisation are required to comply with the procedures contained within this initiative.

Assessing the culture of the organisation

According to Handy's *Understanding Voluntary Organisations* the culture of an organisation is 'The way we do things around here'.

It's the things that are expected; those that are allowed, those that are forbidden. It's the unwritten rule-book that affects the way personnel work and often affects their enjoyment or motivation in their job.

Organisational culture is present in everything the organisation does, particularly in the way it treats:

- the staff from recruitment to retirement
- its clients, customers or users
- the environment and the community

It will be evident through the atmosphere in the workplace how this shows in the level of motivation and the enthusiasm for the task in hand. A culture where everyone keeps their head down and exchanges very little eye contact, except for nervous glances, indicates a negative atmosphere. This is not necessarily an indication of bullying, but may suggest problems in management style.

Identifying the scope of the problem

There are many practical steps one can take to identify the presence of, or potential for, bullying behaviour in an organisation.

Employee surveys

These should be distributed to everyone who works, paid and unpaid, in your organisation, (see Figure 3 on the next page). The purpose is not just to identify bullying behaviour, but to seek information regarding the satisfaction people have in their jobs. The information generated by such a survey, can help to plan training and strategic interventions. The survey should cover elements such as communication, strategy, motivation etc. as well as the presence of bullying behaviour.

It would help to identify problems in management and perhaps highlight the fact that inappropriate and negative behaviour is present.

It is recommended that surveys be completed anonymously, but to allay any 'revealing' fears around the process it may be useful to explain exactly why the survey is being carried out and the relevance of the questions.

Exit interviews

Prepare a form such as the one in Figure 4, ensuring that people have the opportunity to see it and consider the questions, in advance of the interview.

Decide who is carrying out the interviews: a manager, someone from personnel, a committee member or a person external to the organisation.

If conducted consistently and well, exit interviews can produce a good source of reliable data. They can show why people are leaving, how they have viewed their time with your organisation and any specific problems they have experienced.

Although this information will not benefit the leaving employees, it gives you information that may build up some interesting patterns. If you have a serial bully in your midst and these are the most common types, it is likely that certain names will come up repeatedly as being a source of the negative behaviour.

A typical exit interview is shown below, although questions, space and data required may vary.

Figure 3

It is all too easy to make generalisations about the problems that exist in an organisation and to take action without proper information. These questions are designed, therefore, to measure accurately the current situation in a variety of areas concerning both you as an individual and the organisation as a whole. This is very important as it enables an appropriate focus to be made on the most urgent aspects so that real improvements can be implemented. There are no 'right' or 'wrong' answers so try to be as honest and accurate as possible. All information will be treated in the strictest confidence so please do not be influenced by others when you are completing this questionnaire.

Please circle *one* score in each of the following areas as it currently applies to you personally.

Personal criteria	**No problem**				**Overwhelming**
Being managed inappropriately.	1	2	3	4	5
Awareness of roles.	1	2	3	4	5
Personal stress.	1	2	3	4	5
Insufficient resources.	1	2	3	4	5
Insufficient time.	1	2	3	4	5
Unclear goals or strategy.	1	2	3	4	5
Lack of training.	1	2	3	4	5
Lack of motivation.	1	2	3	4	5
Environment (inc. personal space).	1	2	3	4	5
Other (specify).	1	2	3	4	5

Our organisation	**Never**				**Always**
Has a culture of honestly airing interpersonal problems.	1	2	3	4	5
Promotes mutual trust throughout its staff.	1	2	3	4	5
Endeavours to adopt a flexible attitude to problems.	1	2	3	4	5
Provides guidance for self-help.	1	2	3	4	5
Reinforces motivation of staff.	1	2	3	4	5
Communicates all relevant information to its staff.	1	2	3	4	5
Accepts occasional error and learns from it.	1	2	3	4	5
Sticks to an identifiable strategy.	1	2	3	4	5
Says 'thank you' for a job well done.	1	2	3	4	5
Provides adequate and relevant training resources for all of its staff.	1	2	3	4	5
Actively seeks the suggestions and comments of the staff.	1	2	3	4	5
Effectively communicates policy to all its staff.	1	2	3	4	5

Figure 4

Exit Interview

Name ....

Date ....

Duration of employment ....

The purpose of this form is to enable you to present and discuss your own views on your job and how, as an organisation, we have helped or hindered you in the performance of your work. All responses will remain confidential to this process.

What have been the most important achievements during your employment?

Which parts of your work gave you most satisfaction?

Which parts of your work gave you least satisfaction?

What aspects of your own learning have you taken responsibility for?

Which aspects of your job do you feel you could have performed more effectively?

What could have been done that could have improved your performance?

→

Which of your particular skills and abilities were under-used in your job?

What aspects of your job would have benefited from more experience, training or guidance?

Detail the levels of support that have been available to you from:

The organisation

Your line manager

Senior management

Your colleagues

What individual issues, concerns and problems did you feel were not appropriately resolved?

Monitoring staff turnover

If you keep statistics on staff turnover, you can use them to help identify potential trouble spots. You will need to analyse the data and compare results across different departments and units in your organisation, or in small organisations, by comparing figures with other, similar structures.

Examine the results on the basis of the following categories, which can yield significant data:

- The actual number of staff who leave each year.
- The percentage of total staff.
- The numbers in individual departments or units.
- The manager that they reported to.

This can then be used to focus the change process, to help make the case for the instigation of any new culture and provide a starting point for the resolution of the problem.

Once you know what you are dealing with, you are ready, as an organisation, to make a commitment to all employees about what is, and is not, acceptable behaviour in the workplace.

Communicating the organisation's response

Awareness workshops

In order that everyone is aware of the problem, it is important that all staff are able to participate in an initial workshop which highlights the issue and starts to identify the factors around the bullying behaviour.

This is a vital first step that will enable people to acknowledge the potential problem and to recognise the bullying behaviour and the resulting effect on the target. For some people, it will be the first time that they realise that negative management and intolerable working situations actually have a name and a focus.

Newsletters and bulletin boards

Make sure that every opportunity is used to bring people's attention to the initiative. Utilise wall space wherever staff come together, such as cloakrooms, canteens and rest rooms. Include relevant and up-dated information in staff newsletters and handbooks, and let everyone know what the stages are and where the organisation currently stands. Once the initiative is really underway, these media are a vital source of information and give the names of support staff, describe types of unwanted behaviour and so on.

Managers and supervisors

As well as the general information that is available to all staff, make sure that managers and supervisors have a good understanding of the procedures so that they can explain or support their staff initially, if necessary. They may even need training or coaching in listening skills so that they can recognise the potential for problems.

Maintaining the profile

As with many initiatives, the glow of the inception soon fades until it can almost be forgotten. So that the issue is always to the fore, there will need to be regular monitoring and re-evaluation of the current procedures. With the best will in the world, people do forget and the turnover of staff will mean that some people will not have known about the initiative. The organisation should consider including the information in letters of appointment, contracts of employment and as part of staff induction process.

Developing a positive culture initiative

To give the initiative a context and to ensure that it is seen as a valid and integral part of the organisational culture, it will need to develop policies which address this issue.

Although the focus is on workplace bullying, a holistic approach is likely to be more effective, especially in the long-term. Instead of having just a stand alone policy on bullying, this could be part of an overall initiative entitled, 'dignity at work', a phrase, incidently, which derives from European law, whereby harassment and discrimination are examples of unacceptable behaviour which 'affect the dignity of men and women at work'.

Chapter 7

Implementing the Initiative

Formulating a policy

Developing a policy will be the first part of a wider commitment to ensuring a safe, healthy and productive work environment (see Figure 5).

Figure 5

1.0 General
- 1.1 This document is intended as a general proforma for producing a specific and concise written policy.
- 1.2 Careful consideration should be given as to which of the stated criteria in Sections 2.0, 3.0 and 4.0 below will apply to any specific policy and which would therefore need to be included within the policy statement.
- 1.3 Section 5.0 deals with guidelines for implementation of the policy.

2.0 Title
- 2.1 A name for the policy.
- 2.2 An organisational reference or number.
- 2.3 The date of implementation.

3.0 Scope
- 3.1 Acknowledgement that a problem exists which the policy is designed to address.
- 3.2 The personnel to which the policy applies.
- 3.3 Legislation (if any) which the policy addresses.
- 3.4 The formal commitment that the policy will be implemented.
- 3.5 The identification of problems or circumstances specific to the organisation.
- 3.6 Definition of any relevant terminology.

4.0 Objectives
- 4.1 Any specific action required and by whom.
- 4.2 Establish realistic targets with deadlines where appropriate.
- 4.3 Itemised instructions to all designated personnel.
- 4.4 Implementation of rules and/or procedures.
- 4.5 Definition of the monitoring and review process.

5.0 Implementation
- 5.1 Designate a person with overall responsibility for the policy.
- 5.2 Ensure that everyone to whom the policy applies is informed.
- 5.3 Form a small committee or working party to facilitate implementation, monitor progress and review the policy.
- 5.4 Ensure training is available.
- 5.5 Establish achievable goals and realistic timetables.
- 5.6 Formally document all inherent procedures resulting from the policy.
- 5.7 Pursue a culture of constant improvement and strive to change attitudes.
- 5.8 Strive for a positive response by highlighting the benefits.

Reproduced by kind permission of RFC Total Quality Consultancy

A policy is a formal statement of values and an intent to behave in a particular manner. By formulating policies, an organisation makes a public statement of the operation of its staff and procedures and provides a basis and a framework for monitoring and evaluation.

It will be necessary to make a declaration of the type of behaviour the policy addresses. A definition of bullying is a useful starting point, and it should ensure that the organisation has a clear indication of what constitutes bullying.

This document should start with an overall introduction, stating the reasons for its existence, which will be an acknowledgement of the potential for conflict and negative behaviour, and a desire to minimise that risk. There will then be separate sections on bullying, harassment, discrimination, etc. in line with the organisational ethos and emphasis.

In this way, you can update individual sections without having to distribute the entire initiative every time there is a change in procedure or approach.

Formulating your own definition of bullying

You may decide to use or adapt one already in existence such as those noted in the Background chapter, but if that does not entirely meet your needs, or you feel you need to totally 'own' the definition, you will want to devise one of your own. The definition will usually contain a statement noting most or all of the following:

- an example of the types of behaviour, (1)
- the frequency and intensity of the incidents, (2)
- the intent behind the bullying, (3)
- the effects of the behaviour on the target, (4)
- the ultimate outcome of the behaviour, (5).

Example 1

Persistent, (2) offensive, abusive, intimidating, malicious or insulting behaviour, abuse of power or unfair penal sanctions, (1) which make the recipient feel upset, threatened, humiliated or vulnerable, (4) which undermines their self-confidence and which may cause them to suffer stress. (5)

Example 2

Continually (2) threatening and undermining behaviour, (1) expressed in a deliberate (3) and abusive manner, which inappropriately devalues another person's contribution in the workforce, (4) causing them to under-perform and suffer severe stress. (5)

Making a clear statement

The policy should be a clear statement to everyone in the workplace, that certain behaviour is not acceptable and give examples of these, stressing that this list is not exclusive. Examples may be:

- consistent and unwarranted criticism
- imposition of inappropriate 'punishments'
- denying information and resources

The policy will:

- Explain the damaging effects of the behaviour and why it will not be tolerated.
- Outline a recognised and agreed course of action to be taken should any employee behave in an unacceptable manner.
- State that it will be treated as a disciplinary offence.
- Convey that such behaviour may be unlawful, although this is not a criterion for resolution.
- Describe how to get help and to make a complaint.
- Undertake that allegations will be treated speedily, seriously and in confidence.
- Promise protection from victimisation for making a complaint.
- Make it the duty of managers and supervisors to implement the policy and ensure that it is understood.
- Emphasise that all employees carry responsibility for their own behaviour.

The issuing of a policy, however, is not the end of the process. The policy only sets out what will be done and why. Procedures, training, systems etc. all need to be in place to demonstrate the 'how'.

Developing the procedures

The procedures should be devised to enable all staff to be aware of what to do in the case of inappropriate behaviour. Managers and supervisors should receive specific training and assistance in how to invoke and implement a procedure.

Information regarding the procedures should be freely available to all employees, volunteers, sessional staff and others who are involved in the work of your organisation. In addition, guidelines should be devised to enable everyone to access the advice and support services.

Sample guidelines

There are three ways in which complaints can be taken forward, personally, informally and formally. They do not have to be followed in sequence. The objective with all forms of action is to get the unacceptable behaviour to stop.

Personal action

Consideration should be given, in the first instance, to resolving complaints personally. It may be sufficient for the target to raise the matter with the bully, pointing out that their conduct is causing a personal or work-related concern.

Informal action

If this is difficult or embarrassing, the complainant may wish to seek informal help from either their manager, a colleague, personnel or a member of the support team, who can then advise on the options within the policy and the possible outcomes. This meeting may be held away from the normal workplace if this is felt to be necessary or desirable.

Following this meeting, the complainant may wish to talk or write to the bully, to explain that their behaviour is unacceptable. A member of the support team can provide assistance and advice for this action.

If the treatment continues or it is not appropriate to resolve the problem informally, it should be raised through the formal procedure.

Formal action

Where informal methods fail or are inappropriate to the situation, the complainant would be advised to bring a formal complaint. This may involve the assistance of a support team in considering and bringing this complaint forward.

The complaint should be made in writing and where possible include the name of the bully, the type of behaviour complained about, the dates or duration of the behaviour or incidents, names of any witnesses to the behaviour, and action already taken to stop the behaviour.

The complaint will then be sent to an appropriate person, who will appoint a senior manager to investigate.

Supporting the procedures

To assist in the initiative, and to provide support both for the target and the organisation, it may be necessary to involve the services of specialist personnel to carry out certain functions, such as 'contact' or 'support' staff to provide advice and support to the targets of bullying, or witnesses who wish to report an incident, along with investigating officers to determine the facts of the claims.

Training for support staff (example from Fife Council)

Both employee contacts and investigating officers must undergo training before taking on their responsibilities. This initial session is normally of one day's duration for each of the roles and will include an awareness of the issues, the background to the policy and an outline of the proposed implementation.

In addition, the employee contacts will be trained in active listening skills and the investigating officers will cover the disciplinary procedure, outlining the consequences of invoking this and also the levels of censure.

The employee contacts and investigating officers will also have refresher sessions to ensure that the standard of support is maintained and to up-date on any revisions to the policy. They will receive ongoing support from the monitoring group who are drawn from the Human Resources Service, covering employee development, management services, policies, equality and occupational health.

Commitment to all support staff

To encourage the initiative to flourish and to give individuals a sense of trust, the organisation should give employee contacts and investigating officers the following commitments:

- To provide the necessary training to undertake their role.
- To provide time off work and to ensure they do not suffer any penalty in terms of their employment.

- To guarantee that they can, in turn, obtain support where they feel unable to cope with a particular situation.
- To provide appropriate resources to fulfil their role.

Employee contacts

(Adapted from Fife Council's Dignity at Work Policy).

'Employee contacts' provide confidential support to those people who feel they are being harassed in some way and this includes bullying and discrimination. People who face these behaviours at work can find the process of making a complaint very distressing.

Employee contacts are members of council staff who have volunteered to undertake the role. They are recruited with job descriptions and personal specifications and then interviewed in the normal way. Anyone can apply, and every effort is made to ensure the range of contacts is balanced by sex, race, level in the organisation and occupation group.

An employee contact's role is to:

- Listen to an employee who feels they have suffered harassment.
- Discuss the options on a confidential basis.
- Accompany the complainant to talk with the harasser.
- Help the complainant to write to the harasser if requested.
- Accompany the complainant to see their manager or personnel advisor and to meetings within the council arising from the complaint, if requested.
- Continue to support the complainant until council procedures are exhausted.
- Maintain a log of cases dealt with under the policy.
- Attend network meetings with other Employee contacts.
- Attend ongoing training as necessary.

Details of employee contacts will be widely publicised throughout the organisation.

Guidelines on the role of support staff

(Adapted from Cambridge Housing Society Ltd.).

Dealing with initial contact

When approached by a member of staff it is advisable to arrange to discuss their concerns with them as soon as practicable. It is preferable to arrange to meet with them, although they may wish initially to talk the matter through over the telephone.

Meetings should be arranged at a mutually convenient date, time and place, taking into account your work responsibilities. If you are unable to meet with the staff member for any reason e.g. you are going on annual leave, you should suggest that they contact another member of the support staff or the personnel section.

Meetings can be held in work time and on work premises and arrangements must take into account the fact that confidentiality must be maintained.

Your manager must be informed that you will be away from work and advised that you have been requested to act in your role as 'support person'.

Confidentiality

It is important that staff feel that they can discuss their concerns with you in strictest confidence and that any information given will remain confidential between the staff member and yourself.

You should advise the staff member, however, that if you are informed of any serious action which could place tenants, staff or residents at risk, or which involves a crime, you would have an obligation to take the matter further. If this should arise you should refer the matter to personnel. The staff member should be advised that you would not do this without consulting them first.

You should agree from the outset the length of a meeting and it is suggested this should not exceed 45 minutes.

Support offered

It is important to avoid giving advice and avoid saying what you think and feel. Your role is to:

- Encourage the staff member to be responsible for their situation and their decisions.
- Listen to the staff member, to help them think the problem through and talk about how they feel.
- Help the staff member to explore and reflect on the wider context.
- Look at what might have prompted the harassment.
- Consider how the harasser feels about the situation.
- Encourage reflection of the staff member's own behaviour.
- Identify action already taken and to help the staff member think about and decide what to do.

If the staff member decides to use the informal procedure:

- Help the staff member think about what they wish to say to the harasser. It may help to role play discussions.
- Identify other people who could talk to the harasser, their manager, a colleague, personnel.

If the formal procedure is used:

- Help the staff member to put their complaint in writing to the Chief Executive, recording events and actions already taken and identifying evidence to support their case.
- The staff member may ask you to accompany them at their hearing to consider the complaint.

It is not your role to carry out the investigation into an allegation, the Chief Executive will nominate a senior manager to do this.

Investigating a complaint

Sample: 'Statement of Commitment'

The investigator will carry out a thorough investigation within five working days, maintaining confidentiality at all times. All employees involved in the investigation will be expected to respect the need for confidentiality. Failure to do so will be considered a disciplinary offence.

The nominated person will conduct a hearing, see Figure 7, and copies of statements made by witnesses will be made available to the complainant and respondent.

The complainant may be accompanied throughout the procedure and hearing by a member of the support team, a work colleague, a representative of a trade union or another person of their choice.

The respondent will have the right to be accompanied throughout the hearing by a work colleague, a representative of a trade union or another person of their choice.

The person appointed shall consider the facts, including the explanation by the employee regarding the bullying. If the nominated person feels that the bullying has been proved, they will be empowered to take action to resolve the matter.

Guidelines for investigating officers

(Adapted from Fife Council's Dignity at Work Policy).

Investigating Officers will investigate formal complaints of harassment, bullying and discrimination within Fife Council. They will be appointed from across the Council and will have the full delegated authority of the Chief Executive to allow them to fulfil their role.

Investigating Officers will not deal with cases within their own service or area.

The Investigating Officer's role is to:

- Examine all available evidence and conduct interviews with all relevant parties.
- Commence and conclude all investigations as speedily as possible.
- Ensure the investigation is conducted impartially and discreetly.
- Recommend appropriate action and discuss this with the manager.
- Prepare a written report of the outcome, and with a summary stating the complaint, who was interviewed, the main findings and the main recommendations.

Support for support staff

(Example from Cambridge Housing Association Ltd.).

On a four monthly basis meetings with the personnel officer will be arranged for support staff to provide refresher training and briefing sessions. Any further training needs should also be discussed.

Advice can be obtained from personnel at any time on the policy and procedure. When seeking information about individual cases, they should be anonymous in order to safeguard confidentiality.

You will be provided with an information pack, which contains:

- policy and procedures on harassment (staff)
- disciplinary procedure
- grievance procedure
- a copy of the leaflet issued to staff

Investigating a complaint

Establish your terms

Within your written procedures, it will be necessary to decide, beforehand, on the terms you will use for this investigation. It will be more helpful to use unemotive and neutral words such as complainant for the person raising the complaint, whether they are the target or another party, such as a witness to the actions. The respondent is the person who is *responding* to these claims, rather than *accusations*.

Establish your procedure

You will need to decide how the investigation is to be carried out, either by a panel or by an individual. In either case, it is vital that they have been trained or are experienced in skills such as interviewing, analysis and impartial reporting.

Set the scene

Everyone concerned should be encouraged to understand both the confidentiality and the seriousness of the investigation. Tell them how the procedure operates, who is involved and what their role is in the investigation. It will also be useful, at this stage, to state what the outcomes might be.

Emphasise that both parties have a right to attend accompanied by someone else, either a friend or colleague, a contact/support worker or a union representative. This helps them to be more relaxed and possibly less defensive and will give them someone with whom to share reflections later.

Establish the facts

You will probably gather the information in two ways, as a written statement prepared by any or each of the parties and orally at interview.

How you conduct the interviews is very much a matter of choice. You may just allow the parties to give their statement in their own words, or you may wish to use a pro-forma, see Figure 6 as an example, to maintain consistency of approach. You may also like to consider conducting the interviews in the presence of a chosen representative of the parties.

The overall purpose of the interviews is to establish what happened and how. You will need to identify how the respective parties view the actions and the responses to claims and counter-claims. It is important, at all times, that you act impartially as you are there to gather the facts, and not to be swayed by emotion, be it yours or other people's.

Figure 6

Checklist for interviews (Complainant)

Initially, identify and allay any concerns over repercussions resulting from the interview.

Case No. .... **Complainant** ....

Establish:

- What is happening.
- The respondent's role or relationship to the complainant.
- The nature of the behaviour or actions.
- The duration of the behaviour or actions.
- The extent of the behaviour and its context.
- What action they have already taken to address this matter.
- Do other people experience the same behaviour from the respondent?
- What outcome they want from this investigation.
- Is there anything else the complainant wishes to say?
- Assess the emotional and physical state of the complainant.

Name of investigating officer .... Date ....

Checklist for interviews (Respondent)

Case No. .... **Respondent** ....

Explain to the respondent the nature and extent of the claim.

Establish:

- Their response to the claim.

- Their perception of the complainant's behaviour.

- Their perception of their own behaviour.

- Assess the emotional and physical state of the respondent.

- Is there anything the respondent wishes to add?

Name of investigating officer .... Date ....

Checklist for interviews (Witness)

Initially, identify and allay any concerns over repercussions resulting from the interview.

Case No. .... **Witness** ....

Establish:

- Their relationship to the complainant.

- Their relationship to the respondent.

- What are their recollections of the incident or incidents?

- Does the witness have anything to add?

Name of investigating officer .... Date ....

Review the outcomes

After the investigation has taken place, the organisation will need to decide if the claim was legitimate and what happens next to both parties. The exact course of action will be decided by factors such as contractual obligations and working practices, and among the options open are:

- The case is resolved informally, perhaps involving mediation, counselling etc. for either or both parties.
- The respondent is transferred within the organisation.
- Disciplinary action is taken against the respondent.
- The respondent is dismissed.
- The complainant is transferred.

Complete the procedure

- The outcome is notified to the parties in writing.
- Recommendations are made for the next step.

Monitoring and review

The purpose of monitoring is to check the ongoing effectiveness of the policy and its attendant procedures, and to allow improvements to be made where necessary. The monitoring is not intended to check on individuals, but rather the processes, and employees should be assured that the monitoring process will be confidential.

The monitoring will concentrate on the collection of statistical and quantitative information, which should be gathered on a regular basis, from support workers such the employee contacts and investigating officers. The data will include information such as:

- number of complaints or approaches
- number of formal complaints
- outcomes of formal complaints
- types of behaviour leading to complaint

It may also check on the effectiveness of the level of information, by identifying how well people in the organisation are aware of:

- What procedures and sources of help are available to them.
- What is expected of them.
- How to use the procedures.
- How to access sources of help and support.

Information gathered by all forms of investigation should inform amendments to the policy or procedures in consultation with relevant trade unions.

Evaluating the process

All aspects of prevention or resolution of incidents of bullying must be reviewed and evaluated to ensure that everything that can be done has been done. It should ensure that the decision reached was the right one, the actions taken on the basis of that decision were appropriate, and that the procedure is picking up and dealing with all cases. This requires quantitative and qualitative evaluation at various stages, and against both internal and external benchmarks.

In evaluating the effectiveness of the procedures for a resolution of the problem, you may like to consider the following:

- How satisfied are the individuals with the outcomes of the procedures?
- Were both parties allowed the space to tell 'their story' in their own words?
- Do all parties think the procedures fair?
- Do the procedures enable both parties to positively express their emotions such as anger and frustration?
- Are the procedures used as a way of getting revenge?
- Do the procedures serve the interests of parties other than those primarily involved?
- Do the procedures help the parties to solve disputes other than the one at hand?
- Do the procedures and the outcomes of those procedures help to change the culture of the organisation?

You may also wish to ask yourself the following questions:

- What are the costs of the procedures, counted in terms of finance, time, management etc.?
- What are the benefits of the procedures, counted in increased or maintained productivity, levels of emotional and psychological well-being etc.?
- How much do the outcomes satisfy individual and organisational interests?
- What is the effect on relationships within the organisation?
- Do the problems recur?

Other causes of breakdown

After investigation into a particular case, you may decide that it was not, in fact, bullying. There will then need to be an investigation into the background of the case and a decision about the type of behaviour that was actually happening. If current management practices were supposed to be leading, motivating and supporting staff to achieve targets and working *with* them, where did the breakdown occur?

Is this a genuine case of unrealistic or unmatched expectations between the two parties, or is this a case of an unskilled or inexperienced manager needing help, support or training? Either way, it is an organisational responsibility and a place for more senior managers or possibly, the personnel section to offer help to resolve the problem.

Instigate resolution

At this juncture, the complainant may wish to invoke the grievance procedure to resolve this issue.

You will need to ensure that the procedure for handling grievances is understood by the complainant. This procedure should be set out in clear, straightforward language in the employee handbook, as part of a personnel procedures handbook or in a separate document.

Resolution procedure

Should a grievance occur, the employee should be encouraged to raise the issue with their line manager.

If the line manager is unable or unwilling to resolve the issue, the employee, who may be accompanied by a colleague, if desired, can raise the issue with a senior manager or the personnel department. It may be useful at this stage to have the issue put in writing. The employer is advised to ensure that managers and supervisors have been trained to enable them to deal with grievances, and to have a confirmed timetable to deal effectively with the grievance, (see Figure 7).

Figure 7: Sample grievance procedure

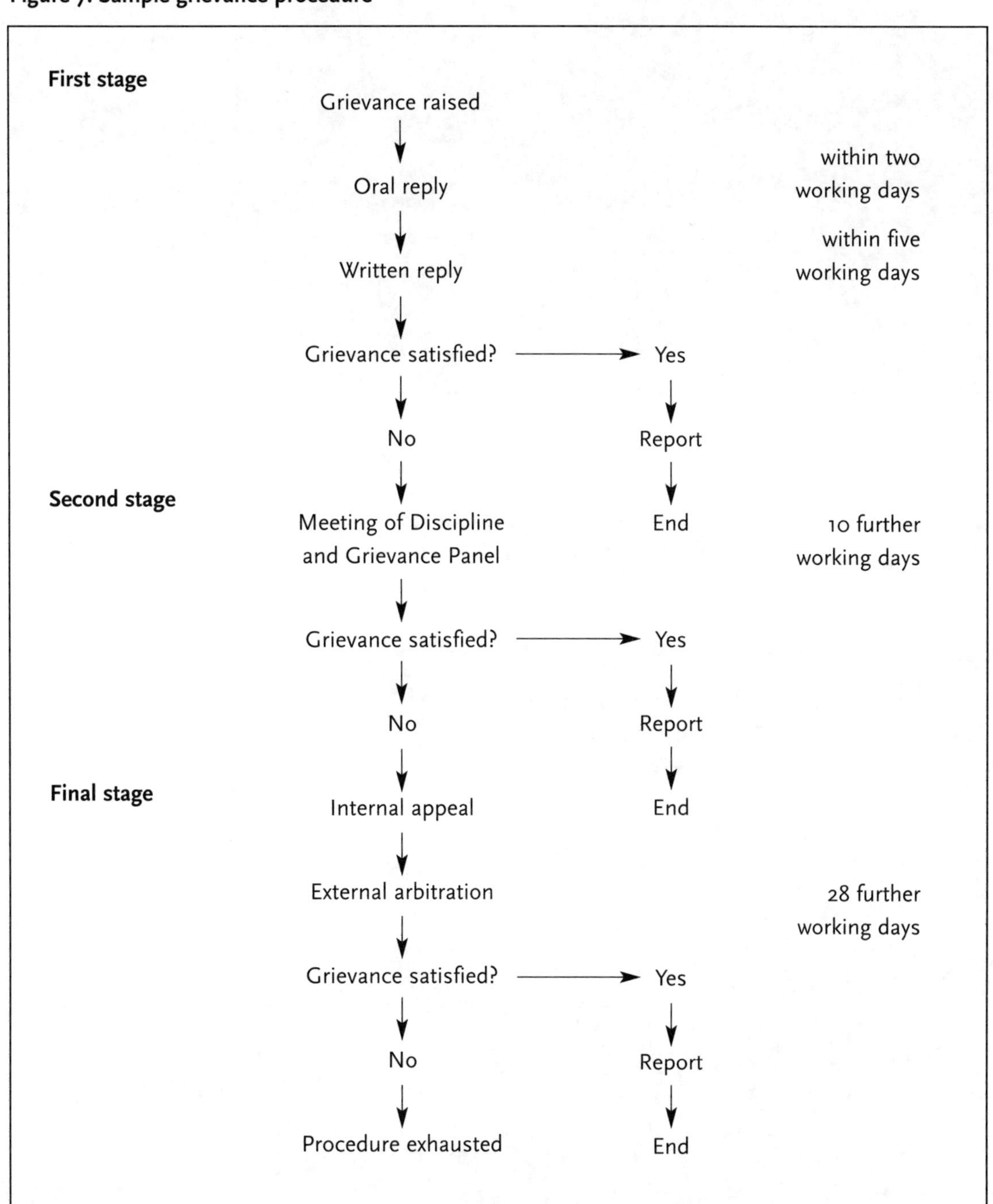

Initiate or improve support systems

It is still quite common for managers to have moved from practitioner posts and received no management training. This creates considerable pressure on the managers and their staff, so you may wish to review and assess the current level of management skills in your organisation.

If the culture has been very isolationist, with very little contact between individuals, teams or units, you may also wish to review the communication and operational systems, such as supervision, appraisal and so on.

An open communication network will reduce the potential for poor management and allow people access to speedier resolution of personal and organisational concerns.

With effective procedures, policies and an overall culture of 'dignity at work', the days of the bully may soon be numbered!

Chapter 8
Organisational Support

At any stage of resolving concerns and complaints about the behaviour of others, you may wish to provide access to supplementary services such as counselling or mediation.

Benefits of counselling

Counselling is a positive process, which can help to protect the individual within an organisation, as well as foster a climate of trust and openness. It is especially useful when dealing with cases of bullying, as it can be used to give the target an opportunity to establish the extent of the situation and respond positively to the bully. It can also support both bully and target when they return to the workplace and this will be especially important if the case is not proven.

The counsellor may be part of the organisation or they may be external. In both cases they must be:

- respected
- well regarded
- trusted
- credible
- well-trained

By using a counselling approach, an organisation creates the environment to identify and clarify issues and confirm the reliability and status of the reports.

For the target it can also:

- Allow them to confront and overcome their fear.
- Help them to look for positive solutions.
- Work to regain self-esteem.
- Develop their self-reliance and tackle their feelings of powerlessness.
- Provide support in making decisions and carrying through any responses.

Although this service is a primary support to the target, the counselling should be available to both parties. Through counselling, the bully may also wish to explore ways of changing their behaviour and to examine the implications of that behaviour. They may also need support to re-enter the workplace and work with the target.

Helpful approaches

Before moving onto any remedial work, the counsellor will need to establish the target's desired outcome from the sessions. Do they wish to gain the strength to confront the bully or only support through the sessions? If they want support to face the bully the counsellor will help by:

- Encouraging them to communicate clearly by stating exactly how they feel because of the bully's behaviour.
- Using role-play to take them through a scenario, which can help them to rehearse what they want to say.
- Encouraging them to be objective about the situation, so that if they wish to make a formal complaint later, they have the facts clear.
- Encouraging them to imagine their work environment if the bullying ceased.
- Focussing on projecting a positive workplace, with them being in control of their own life.
- Helping them to consider other sources of support such as assertiveness and stress management workshops.
- Helping them to evaluate in advance their reactions if things do not turn out as they hope.

Considerations

Introducing a counselling service into an organisation where such facilities were previously unknown may raise suspicions and concerns. Before its introduction, as a fait accompli, it would be wise to consider the following, so that you have responses in place to address any doubts about its effectiveness.

- Employees may doubt that the process will help or even work successfully, including serious doubts about the effectiveness of the confidentiality element.
- Trade unions may not see it as an impartial operation and decide not to support it.
- Managers may be wary of the process, believing it might encourage frivolous and unnecessary use, 'giving in to weak staff' and encouraging a culture of absenteeism.

The structure, and the procedures within the structure will need to be carefully planned and evaluated before the implementation of the service. Serious consideration must be given to its location, costs, and management, since, if these elements are not properly evaluated, the service may not have the stability and sustainability needed to make it an effective and valued service.

Benefits of mediation

In many cases a successful resolution can be achieved at the end of informal discussions or a formal investigation. For some organisations facing what may seem to be an impossible or improbable outcome, with the two parties working together in harmony again, mediation may be one means to a solution.

Some organisations may even consider mediation without moving to any formal investigation, as they feel it will save money and time. It may also save 'face' for those involved, most of whom will be glad of a way out that stops the bullying and harassment. Mediation helps the parties to agree a course of action and a solution, but it must be adapted to the needs of the organisation.

The purpose of mediation is to assist parties who have a conflict or disagreement and to enable them to reach a stage where the conflict can be resolved in a permanent manner, rather than 'settled', which is only a temporary measure.

The process of mediation needs a voluntary agreement that all parties will abide by the course of action and the agreed solution. It is without prejudice and all notes of individual cases must be destroyed when it ends. Confidentiality is paramount in both the agreement and in the independent and joint meetings with the parties involved.

The process also requires consensual parties since it won't work if people won't compromise.

The mediator?

To gain the most objectivity and trust, it is advisable to have someone external to the organisation, such as a professional mediator or an independent consultant.

However, it is possible to involve a trained or experienced person from within your own organisation, but it will need to be one that is far removed from either parties, say, someone from another site or campus.

Their purpose is not to judge but to help to find a solution that is acceptable to both parties, that is voluntary, and allows each to retain dignity.

The mediator is a facilitator, and manages the process, not the content. That means that they allow each party to be significant contributors to the process, whilst safeguarding their own neutrality.

The mediator must have immunity, and cannot be called as a witness.

Procedure

Mediation works in a similar way to other negotiation processes and will involve the following elements.

As preparation, set up a comfortable environment in a room with no 'negative memories, so do not use a manager's office if it has been the scene of a bullying incident. Supply the usual comforts such as tea, coffee, water, tissues and so on. A review of all available background material will be needed.

Throughout, there should be an openness preferably with both parties present and the complainant accompanied by friend, colleague or TU representative.

There will be a comprehensive introduction of the issues, on paper and without interruption, followed by a broad private meeting with the separate parties to gauge feelings, moving on to concerns from the past and towards the future.

The mediation will be looking for solutions such as 'I just want an apology and to get on with my job', or 'I can't work with this person again', and trying to find common ground. At this stage the parties need to think about how they viewed the situation then and now, and this may be done with each party separately or together. The common feature should be that they *are* seeking common ground.

If the participants really want a solution, mediation should take no longer than one day. For those who are unsure of the process or who lack confidence in its effectiveness, more time may be necessary. These vagaries should be addressed beforehand by writing the mediation procedure into the Dignity at Work Policy and including:

- The methods of monitoring and enforcing agreements.
- The nature of the mediator, who should be external to the organisation or department.
- How mediators will be selected and trained, where meetings will take place, outlining the facilities and resources to be provided.
- The administration procedure.
- The monitoring procedure.
- The involvement of the trade union.

The role and function of the mediator

The mediator's main task is to help the parties to move the conflict forward, but they may also try to achieve empowerment or mutual recognition. These aims will affect how the mediator approaches the conflict, the methods they follow and the options they offer. The mediator should leave the way open for the parties to the conflict to move beyond the conflict and to acknowledge the validity of the other's concerns.

The mediator must also walk a tightrope between being too structured and being too responsive. Too much structure will cause the participants to feel they are locked into a process in which they are not listened to and consequently not playing an effective role, but rather that the process is being dictated to them. On the other hand, too much pliancy will make the parties to the conflict risk feeling that they are playing out the conflict over and over again.

The mediator must remain neutral, balanced, and yet be involved in a way that does not favour either party.

There is no one best way to mediate, and the mediation style will be determined by the issue, the parties, the deadline and so on. The right way is the way that works.

Establishing rapport

It is helpful to remind the parties to the conflict of the agreed-upon ground rules and this is a perfect illustration of why the parties and not the mediator should establish the ground rules, since the risk in not doing this is to make the offending party feel wrong and alienated.

To make progress, a mediator needs to establish a good rapport with the parties to the dispute. This may be achieved by:

- Physical matching, where the mediator tries to match 50 per cent of each party's physical posture and gestures.
- Checking every few minutes to make sure that they are physically in tune with the parties and perhaps changing posture to reflect that of the non-speaking party.

Once the mediator has established a physical rapport with the parties, it is easier to gently 'lead' the parties to follow a lead in whatever direction the mediator may wish to go.

If the participants feel fully understood, then work with them becomes most effective.

Language

To help all parties to explore the situation, the following phrases may be appropriate:

- I appreciate that you...
- What are your concerns?
- What do you mean by 'everything'?
- How do you define 'fair'?
- What do you think would happen if...?
- If you could have it the way you want. How would that be?
- Do you see any other way to resolve the issue?
- I feel that you seem to have come to agreement on this.

Outcomes

To give a focus to the discussion, the mediator will want to pose an 'outcome question', that is a 'What do you want' question, phrasing this question in a number of ways:

- What do you hope to achieve through mediation?
- Why are you in mediation?
- What do you expect the results to be?
- How would you like the outcome to be?
- How do you see the issues being best resolved?
- How will you know when the result has been achieved?
- How will you know when the outcome is fair?
- On what basis would you be prepared to agree?
- What will you need to agree?
- What type of agreement would you like to reach?

Satisfaction

In mediation, the parties to the dispute are looking for some sort of satisfaction. This satisfaction may take one or more of the following forms:

- Clearly communicating certain issues to the other party.
- Wanting the other party to acknowledge certain perspectives or feelings.
- The need to comprehensively consider all the options.

Resolutions

Throughout the mediation process there will be a repeat and rephrasing of what each party to the conflict wants the resolution to be. There might also be a sort of conditional close periodically by saying that 'if x takes place then y will be considered to be resolved. Is that correct?'

The mediator will also need to make the parties understand that while not all issues will be resolved perfectly, steps have been taken to ensure that progress is being made.

They may want to use quotes, analogies or metaphors to facilitate the process, and speak of the mediation as a journey and not a battle, with terms such as 'beginning', 'middle' and 'end' or 'steep paths' or 'rough water'.

To help the parties to the conflict to see that other people have been through similar circumstances and have now resolved their conflicts, the mediator may use analogies that are relevant to what the parties currently do for a living. They can use statements such as 'some people preferred to do this' or 'lots of people have found that this worked'.

The role of the mediator, then, can be summed up as:

- **Convenor:** Contacting the parties to arrange meeting and times.
- **Educator:** Educating the parties about the purpose, options and limits of mediation.
- **Communication facilitator:** Ensuring that all parties to the conflict are heard.
- **Translator:** Rephrasing or re-communicating messages.
- **Questioner and clarifier:** Making sure that the mediation stays on track by questioning the parties and by clarifying their responses.
- **Process advisor:** Explaining the process of mediation and ensuring that all parties participate.
- **Catalyst:** Offering options, alternatives, perspectives and points for consideration.
- **Recorder:** Keeping records of the meetings and noting the progress made in each one.

The techniques of the mediator include:

- Restating what has been said and feeding it back to the parties in their own words.
- Paraphrasing, which creates some neutrality by blurring the edges of what has actually been said.
- Decoding a message and feeding it back to the emotions of the parties.
- Summarising and condensing the message.
- Generalising the points that parties have made.
- Expanding on what the parties have said and sending it back to them.
- Putting the parties' thoughts and comments into some order or sequence.
- Helping each speaker to structure their thoughts.
- Separating and dividing the comments into smaller sections for easier understanding.

Encouraging objectivity

Backtracking: one way of making sure that the parties retain their emotional state is for the mediator to summarise what they have been saying, when they will listen in order to make sure that they have not been misrepresented.

Normalisation: it is often helpful for the participants to a conflict to be reminded that other people have been in a similar situation and that their situation has been resolved.

Separation: it is important that the mediator separates the person and the problem, by differentiating between past focused relational/emotional issues and the person's future-based goals.

Mediation has been used in the business world for many years when two parties can't agree and can't see a way out of a conflict. It is usually employed in sales or compensation cases to come to a satisfactory resolution. Its use in employment issues is relatively new, but growing. It is, however, a powerful tool and therefore requires trained and experienced people to be involved in its implementation.

The Legal Aspects

The current employment position

At present, there is no *single* law which can be invoked to encourage employers to take positive action on the issue of bullying. Nor can a bullied individual easily extract redress for the intentional negative behaviour of another, which causes them extreme stress and damage. Within the European Union currently, only Sweden has specific anti-bullying laws.

Further:

- The incidence and evidence of bullying in the workplace is increasing.
- The health and safety aspects indicate that an increasing amount of time at work is lost through bullying, due to the effects of stress on the target and those who witness it.
- The existing anti-discriminatory legislation concerning inappropriate behaviour focussing on sex, race and disability does not cover bullying.
- The constructive dismissal legislation is not particularly helpful to targets of bullying as it does not recognise that most people want to keep their jobs.

But all is not complete doom and gloom. Employees who are being bullied can pursue action under certain sections of a variety of British laws, which may be used to extract some protection.

Employment Protection (Consolidation) Act 1978

To qualify under this Act, the employee must satisfy four criteria:

- They must have been employed for a continuous 52 weeks to be eligible for unfair dismissal.
- They must establish that they have been dismissed by the employer, or have been constructively dismissed.
- The reasons for dismissal were not 'fair' within the scope of the law, including misconduct, drunkenness or violence.
- The employer had not acted reasonably.

With constructive dismissal, the employee must be able to show that conditions of work were so intolerable that he or she had no choice but to resign under Section 55 (2) (C). This states:

> *'an employee shall be treated as dismissed by his employer…if the employee terminates that contract with or without notice in circumstances such that he is entitled to terminate it without notice by reason of the employer's conduct'.*

For an employee to bring a successful action of constructive dismissal against an employer the employee must prove that:

- The bullying was the equivalent of a breach of contract.
- The breach caused the resignation.

- The breach was serious enough to justify the employee resigning.
- The employee did not delay too long in resigning. A delay may mean that the worker has waived the breach.

If an employee files for dismissal on the grounds of constructive dismissal the claim must be lodged with the Employment Tribunal within three months of leaving the job.

If the bullying results in physical or psychological injury the employee may be entitled to damages. However, to win a claim for damages the target must show:

- The bullying caused the employee actual physical injury or a medically recognised psychological ailment.
- The employer knew that the bullying was likely to cause injury (i.e. the employer had been warned by the target).
- The employer failed to take reasonable steps to prevent it.

Because of the responsibilities placed on an employer, where the bully makes it impossible for the employee to carry out their duties, this is considered a major breach of trust and confidence. This breach of trust is considered a breach of contract as there exists an implied duty 'for the employer to prove reasonable support to enable a worker to carry out their duties without disruption or harassment from fellow employees'.

However, as legislation currently stands, a situation must become unbearable before an employee resigns.

Health and Safety at Work Act 1974

The Act sets out five areas of duties for employers where they must:

- Provide a safe place and system of work.
- Ensure safety in the use of dangerous materials and substances.
- Maintain a safe place of work including access to the place of work.
- Provide a safe working environment.
- Provide information, instruction, training and supervision to ensure the safety of employees.

Section 2 also states, 'It shall be the duty of every employer to ensure so far as is reasonably practicable the health, safety and welfare at work of its employees.'

The subsequent Act of 1998 applies to psychological as well as physical well-being and includes the protection from excessive stress.

This means, in practice, that if the bully makes it impossible for the target then the employer has breached the contract of confidence and trust.

The Health and Safety at Work Act 1974, Sections 2 and 3, together with the Management of Health and Safety at Work Regulations 1992 requires employers to ensure the health and safety of employees and others affected by their work activities and to conduct an assessment of the risks to which employees are exposed.

Employment Rights Act 1994

This enables employees to take a case to an employment tribunal if they believe they have been constructively dismissed for example, or if an employer has failed to protect the target of bullying and the target feels they have no action but to resign to escape the bullying.

Sex Discrimination Act 1975, Race Relations Act 1976

If there is a racial or sexual element to the bullying the employer can be held vicariously liable. In this case, the employee does not have to have been employed for two years.

Protection from Harassment Act 1997

This Act is not aimed primarily at employment but its provisions may afford a legal remedy to employees on areas not currently covered by law e.g. age, religious beliefs, political persuasion, sexual orientation and bullying.

It does, however, cover 'stalking' and enables employees to take civil action when a colleague's actions amount to harassment.

Significantly, the Protection from Harassment Act accords emphasis for the first time on the target's *perception* of the harassment rather than the perpetrator's alleged intent.

Disability Discrimination Act 1995

This makes it illegal to discriminate against a disabled person at work on account of their disability. It covers an employee who has suffered discrimination or victimisation or who has been treated less favourably than other employees as a result of a disability or impairment.

The Criminal Justice and Public Order Act 1994

This Act makes it an offence to use threatening, abusive or insulting words or behaviour. It covers cases where one person acts with intent to cause another person harassment, alarm or distress by the use of threatening, abusive or insulting words or behaviour.

Using the law

At present, the area of law concerned with bullying is civil law, which deals with the rights and duties between citizens and businesses. The outcome of this kind of law is compensatory, not punitive, as in criminal law.

If you feel you are the target of bullying and your employer is doing nothing about it, you may wish to go to an employment tribunal which is an independent judicial body consisting of a legally qualified chair and two lay members.

If you are bringing the case to the tribunal, you are known as the applicant. The person or organisation against whom you are bringing the case is the respondent. It may be advisable to cite the organisation as the first respondent and the individual as the second respondent.

As the plaintiff, you can prepare and present your case without a solicitor. Obviously, if you feel that you are not able to tackle that, contact a solicitor, who can take your case on a no-win, no-fee basis. Remember that your solicitor will need your medical records, so make sure that you keep your GP informed of what is happening, and which means you need to have consulted them on this particular issue.

At the tribunal, each party is responsible for their respective costs. But you may be asked to pay costs if the tribunal feels you have acted in a 'frivolous, vexatious, abusive, disruptive or unreasonable' manner, and if you lose the case, you may have to pay the other side's costs, so it is worthwhile to take out insurance against this. The Law Society Personal Injury Panel can advise you on this.

Tribunals can make legally binding decisions in areas of employment-related cases and can enable people to take cases to court without having to go through the time and cost of going to a higher court. At the time of writing, the maximum that a tribunal can award is £20,000.

When you are applying to have your case heard, and after you have filled in the necessary paperwork, the tribunal will contact ACAS, who will see if an agreement can be reached by the two parties. As ACAS's services are free, you can contact them before you go to the tribunal.

The tribunal may insist on a pre-hearing review, if it feels the case is weak.

Tribunals have the power to order an employer to reinstate an employee. This rarely happens and, given events, may not always be the wisest course of action.

The Health and Safety at Work Act has extended existing legislation and set up an executive, which is responsible for inspecting and prosecuting offending companies. This action is not available to individuals.

The employer's contractual obligations

When employees start work, they enter into a contract of employment with the employer. The contract may be written or implied, but it lays certain obligations on each, and these obligations are in force as soon as an offer of work is given and accepted. Within the terms of contract, there are two elements:

- **Express:** these are the legal requirements, which usually cover pay, hours, duties, sick pay etc.
- **Implied:** these expect that an employee must exercise reasonable skill and care in their duties and obey reasonable instructions.

There are also terms inserted by statute as part of every contract, which state that all employees, regardless of how many hours they work each week, or how long they have worked, have certain basic rights:

- Not to be discriminated against.
- Not to be unfairly dismissed.
- To be given written reasons for dismissal.
- To be given redundancy pay.

- Health and safety rights.
- The right to belong to a trade union.
- The right to information.
- Other rights such as statutory sick pay.

Future legislation

The MSF Union, who have taken a prominent role in lobbying for legislation to protect targets of bullying, promoted the Dignity at Work Bill in 1996. Drafted by employment law experts Thompsons, it was introduced into the House of Lords as a private member's Bill by Lord Monkswell at the end of that year.

Although the Bill did not become law, due to lack of parliamentary time, awareness was raised on the need for legislation to contain and address this problem.

The Dignity at Work Bill (Clause 1) sets out very clearly the acts that infringe dignity at work and includes:

- Repeated behaviour which is offensive, abusive, malicious, insulting or intimidating.
- Repeated unjustified criticism.
- Detrimental changes to the employee's duties or responsibilities without reasonable justification.

This Bill enables employees to use legal means to deal with bullying at work and provides employers with a framework to take positive steps to deal with the issue.

The steps the employer must take are:

- Adopting, implementing and enforcing a dignity at work policy.
- Repudiating acts of bullying within three working days after a complaint.
- Remedying the loss, damage or detriment suffered by the person making the complaint.

A case for bullying must be brought within 90 days of dismissal. Late applications will be allowed, but it must be proved that it was 'not reasonably practical' to bring the case before.

You may also need to seek specialist advice on the relevance of The Human Rights Act (1998) and The Employment Relations Act (1999) in particular cases of bullying.

References

Adams, A. and Crawford, N. (1992) *Bullying at Work*, Virago.

Curtis, L. (1993) *Harassment, Stalking and Assault-making Advances: What you can do About Sexual Harassment at Work*, BBC Books.

Earnshaw, J. and Cooper, C. (1996) *Stress and Employer Liability*, IPD.

Field, T. (1996) *Bully in Sight*, Success Unlimited.

Ford, K. and Hargreaves, S. (1991) *First Line Management; Staff*, Harlow, Longman.

Handy, C. (1988) *Understanding Voluntary Organisations*, Pelican.

Health and Safety Executive (1995) *Stress at Work: A Guide for Employers*, HMSO.

Honey, P. (1980) *Solving People Problems*, McGraw Hill.

Hope, P. and Pickles, T. (1995) *Performance Appraisal*, Lyme Regis, Russell House Publishing.

Hunt, G. (1998) *Whistleblowing*, London, Arnold.

Independence Educational Publishers, Child and Adult Bullying, *Bullying Issues*, v13, Cambridge, Independence Educational Publishers.

Institute of Management (1996) *Dealing with Bullying at Work in a Week*, Hodder and Stoughton.

Institute of Personnel and Development (1994) *Survey on Bullying in the Workplace*, I.P.D.

Ishmael, A. with Alemoru, B. (1999) *Harassment, Bullying and Violence at Work*, Industrial Society.

Kinchin, D. (1998) *Stress, PTSD and Psychiatric Injury*, Success Unlimited.

McCarthy, Sheehan, and Wilkie (Eds.), (1996) *Bullying: From Backyard to Boardroom*, Millennium Books.

Morrison, C. A. (1991) *The RTI Practical Guide to Supervision*. Research Training Initiative.

Namie, G. and Namie, R. (1999) *Bullyproof Yourself at Work! Personal Strategies to Stop the Hurt from Harassment*, DoubleDoc Press.

Randall, P. (1996) *Adult Bullying: Perpetrators and Victims*, Routledge.

Raynor, C. (1994) *The Incidence of Workplace Bullying*, Staffs University Business School.

Stevens, T. (1999) *Bullying and Sexual Harassment*, Institute of Personnel Development.

Taylor, G. and Thornton, C. (1995) *Managing People*, Directory of Social Change.

Taylor, G. (1996) *Employment Practice Guidelines*, Federation of Independent Advice Centres.

Taylor, G. (1996) *Managing Recruitment and Selection,* Directory of Social Change.

Vinton, G. (1994) *Whistleblowing: Subversion or Corporate Citizenship?* London, Paul Chapman Publishing.

Wheatley, R. (1999) *Dealing with Bullying at Work in a Week*, Institute of Management.

Sources of Help and Advice

The following information is just a selection of the sources that can be approached to find out more about the issue of workplace bullying.

In addition to publications available from most bookshops, those with access to the internet may wish to view the many new websites, coming on line daily. Once you tap into one, you can find links to others that should give you the information you require.

Andrea Adams Trust
Maritime House,
Basin Road North,
Hove
East Sussex BN4 1WA
Tel/fax 01273 704900
email aat@btinternet.com
You can also obtain the video made by The TUC and The Industrial Society on workplace bullying, by contacting The Trust – £795 (preview available).

Campaign Against Bullying At Work (CABAW)
Chris Ball,
MSF Centre,
33-37 Moreland Street,
London EC1V 8BB
Tel 020 7505 3000

Public Concern At Work
Tel 020 7404 6609
Lincoln's Inn House,
42 Kingsway,
London WC2B 6EN
Provides free advice to employees on whistleblowing, fraud, abuse, corruption, health and safety.

UK Work Stress Network
Tel/fax 01603 868249.
Brian Robinson, Convenor,
9 George Road,
Drayton,
Norwich NR8 6ED
Publishes UK National Work-stress Network News.
Editor Ian Draper, NASUWT,
9 Bell Lane,
Syresham,
Brackley NN13 5HP
Tel 01280 850388
Fax 01280 850056

REDRESS:The Bullied Teachers' Support Network
Tel 01405 764432
Fax 01405 769868
Jenni Watson, Secretary,
REDRESS,
Bramble House,
Mason Drive,
Hook
DN14 5NE

Helplines

UK National Workplace Bullying Advice Line
Tel 01235 834548 (recorded message with instructions)
Fax 01235 861721
Tim Field provides information relating to bullying for employees, employers, support organisations, unions, counsellors, researchers, media, etc. Contact Tim to obtain information sheet and newsletter.

Workplace Bullying Information Line
Tel 0131 339 9232 Tuesday 7-9pm and Saturday 10am-midday.
Scotland's helpline for employees and employers: run by Sandra Brown.
http://members@aol.com/sandra7510/

The Andrea Adams Trust
Tel 01273 704900. The office is normally staffed between 10am and 4pm weekdays.

Bullied at Work Helpline
Gill Rowe: 01242 820213 Monday-Friday 1pm-7pm or Sundays 10am-12noon
http://www.epinet.co.uk/bullying email Rowe.Whalfarm@farmline.com
Based in Gloucestershire, but available UK wide for advice and counselling relating to workplace bullying and harassment.

Fay Fielding
Tel 01422 882258
North of England based, provides an informal telephone service to people experiencing bullying at work, especially teachers, and is normally available weekday evenings between 6pm-8pm and mornings at the weekend.

Bully Alert UK
Tel 01227 277993
Especially for those in the NHS and voluntary sector.

Janet Samuel's Imperative
Tel 020 8885 1677 Monday-Tuesday 7pm-9pm, Saturday 9.30am-11.30am.
Bullying support line

Campaign Against Bullies At Work
Tel 01226 285103 between 7pm-9pm Monday-Friday
Yorkshire-based helpline

Tribunals Helpline
Tel 0345 959775.

Support groups

BALM (Bullied and Abused Lives in Ministry)
http://wwwbalmnet.co.uk
BALM offers support to church ministers and their close family.

HSG (formerly Huntingdon Support Group)
Tel 01480 462938
To help tackle corporate bullying. They can assist you in identifying the bullying techniques used in public or large private sector corporations, with particular experience in dealing with local authority bullying.

Oxfordshire employees Bullied Out of Work (OXBOW)
Jennie Chesterton, 01367 710308 or Nigel Martindale, 01869 241932
A support group for people who are being or have been bullied. Consisting mostly (but not exclusively) of teachers, ex-teachers and ex-social workers, the group meets in Oxford.

Freedom to Nurse
freedomtonurse@yahoo.com
PO Box 37, Worksop,
Notts S80 1ZT.
A group run by and for grassroots nurses to offer support to nurses who are bullied when they try and tackle problems at work. Survival Guide available.

Teachers Against Bullying
Primary teachers contact: Teresa Mcmahon at 00 3531 288 3062, between 7pm and 9pm. Secondary teachers contact: Norman Wilson by email – wilsonn@gofree.indigo.ie
To help teachers who have been, or are being bullied out of school with the purpose to help relieve the feelings of isolation.

Organisations and individuals

Arbitration, Conciliation and Advisory Services (ACAS)
27 Wilton Street,
London SW1X 7AZ
The national body for arbitration and employment matters. Information and assistance can be obtained from local offices throughout the UK. Telephone numbers available locally. They have also published two advisory leaflets on bullying entitled *Bullying and Harassment at Work*, one for employees and the other for managers and employers. (ACAS Reader Service: Tel 0145 585 2225).

British Association of Counselling
Tel 01788 578328
Fax 01788 562189
1 Regent Place,
Rugby,
Warwickshire CV21 2PJ
Supplying information and lists of recognised counsellors.

Campaign against Bullying
Tel 00 3531 288 7976
email odonnllb@indigo.ie
http://www.clubi.ie/killick/cab/
Vivette O'Donnell,
72 Lakelands Avenue,
Stillorgan
Co Dun Laoighaire/Rathdown

The Council for Academic Freedom and Academic Standards (CAFAS)

Colwyn Williamson, Tel 01792 295895
University College, Fax 01792 295893
Swansea SA2 8PP

Central Office of the Industrial Tribunals Tel 01284 762300
100 Southgate Street,
Bury St Edmunds,
Suffolk IP33 2AQ,

Concerned Spouses of Suffering/Stressed Teachers (COSST) Tel 0114 287 3087
Peter Lewis,
22 Marlborough Rise,
Aston, Sheffield S26 2ET
A self-help and mutual support organisation for partners of stressed teachers. (Enclose sae when making enquiry.)

Countering Bullying Unit Tel 01222 506532
Delwyn Tattum, Faculty of Education and Sport, Fax 01222 747665
University of Wales Institute Cardiff,
Cyncoed Centre,
Cyncoed Road,
Cardiff CF2 6XD
Focus on bullying in schools and prisons. Publications available.

Employment Tribunal
For a free booklet on the Tribunal procedure call the UK ET Helpline on 0345 959775

Equal Opportunities Commission Tel 0161 833 9244
Overseas House, Fax 0161 835 1657
Quay Street,
Manchester M3 3HN

Freedom To Care Tel/fax 020 8224 1022
PO Box 125, email freedomtocare@aol.com
West Molesey,
Surrey KT8 1YE
A UK organisation for whistleblowers and their supporters, with links to similar campaigners in Australia.

Health and Safety Executive Tel 0114 289 2345
HSE Information Centre, Fax 0114 289 2333
Broad Lane,
Sheffield S3 7HQ

Institute of Personnel and Development Tel 020 8971 9000
IPD House, Fax 020 8263 3244
Camp Road,
London SW19 4UX
The professional body for personnel officers and human resource management.

International Harassment Network Tel 01584 877700

Vicki Merchant,
19 The Bull Ring,
Ludlow,
Shropshire SY8 1AA
Fax 01584 874400
email Merchant.v@dial.pipex.com
http://dspace.dial.pipex.com/merchant,v/
A commercial organisation, working with employers to tackle bullying and harassment.

The Centre for Personal and Professional Development
Tel 01962 715838
Fax 01962 715160
Ann Williams,
The Mill,
Shawford,
Winchester,
Hampshire SO21 2BP
Provides counselling, consultancy and training services for individuals and organisations, specialising in workplace issues.

Bill Reynolds
Tel 01280 823811
Fax 01280 823822
Independent Advocates,
PO Box 1832,
Buckingham MK18 1NZ
Bill Reynolds is an independent advocate with experience of tribunals that involve bullying. If you're considering taking legal action against bullying, Bill is willing to offer up to two hours of telephone advice or one hour of advice at his office without charge.